Teaching Notes on Piano Examination Pieces 2001–2002

Grades 1–7

CLARA TAYLOR
FRAM FRSA LRAM

Chief Examiner of
The Associated Board of the Royal Schools of Music

ANTHONY WILLIAMS
MMUS DIPRAM GRSM LRAM

Head of Keyboard and Assistant Director of Music at Radley College

Teaching Notes on Piano Examination Pieces 2001–2002

Grades 1–7

The Associated Board of the Royal Schools of Music

First published in 2000 by
The Associated Board of the Royal Schools of Music (Publishing) Limited
14 Bedford Square, London WC1B 3JG, United Kingdom

ISBN 1 86096 157 6

AB 2756

A CIP catalogue for this book is available from The British Library.

Printed in England by Halstan & Co. Ltd, Amersham, Bucks

CONTENTS

INTRODUCTION

Teachers reading the commentaries and general hints in this booklet will realize that they were written with personal understanding of the many challenges that teachers face. Having taught at all levels, from beginners to diploma standard, Anthony Williams and I are very much aware of the skill, patience and insight needed to help average pupils along the way. Musically talented, motivated children are a joy and present fewer difficulties to their fortunate teachers but these pupils are in a minority. The Associated Board's system of grades is for the benefit of all levels of ability and was originally intended for those who form the vast majority of candidates heard in exams throughout the world.

The exciting increase in the number of pieces for each grade not only enlivens the teacher's work but also makes it possible to find a programme that really suits each individual candidate. Do explore the pieces that are not printed in the graded albums; these are easily obtainable and there are some wonderful choices in these lists that might otherwise be missed. In the commentaries we hope to have given sufficient guidance to enable you to suit the pieces to your own students with even more awareness and confidence than before. The first essential in starting a new piece is the desire to learn it. Once a pupil's interest is caught, the business of managing the musical and technical essentials becomes purposeful and more easily sustained. We have tried to suggest angles of approach, especially in repertoire that does not have an imaginative title. So often it is the way in which the music is introduced to the pupil that influences the effort that follows and we have often given priority to these considerations.

In giving information about phrasing, dynamics and fingering, we stress that these are suggestions based on experience. Teachers will all have their own ideas and we have tried to avoid being fussily prescriptive. In the choice of fingering in particular, so much depends on each individual pupil and the final question to ask will always be: 'Does it work easily and create the right musical effect?'

Perhaps it should be emphasized that in pointing out what examiners will be listening for we are only suggesting ways of benefiting the music. Anything that improves the performance is bound to be welcomed in the exam and it is, after all, the standard of playing and love of music that count in the long run.

It may be useful to consider the following areas in more detail.

1

TEMPO

Slow practice is often essential but it pays to keep the final performing tempo of the piece in mind. Sometimes pupils get stuck at a slow pace, use too heavy a touch and find it difficult to achieve the fluency and vitality of faster repertoire. Cautious players need particular encouragement and plenty of demonstration to give a clear sound picture of the intended speed. The same applies to scales and arpeggios, where an even tone and a good flowing tempo are both important.

RUBATO

This is an unmistakable element in musical phrasing but can also be encouraged by explanation to less-naturally-aware pupils. In Classical or earlier styles, the small fluctuations are within the bar and need to be very subtle indeed to avoid upsetting the basic pulse. Phrasing in these styles is shown more effectively by the use of tone, gently emphasizing the main points and being aware of the rise and fall of the pitch. *Rubato* in Romantic styles shapes the phrases by moving towards the main peak, then relaxing afterwards. Pupils are often better at making a *ritardando* than at getting faster but both forms of movement are needed to create balanced phrasing. Picking up the tempo after a *ritardando* is also a skill that needs awareness. Pencilling in arrows pointing forwards and backwards in the music is often a helpful way of giving visual clues and encouraging the pupil to look ahead. Even experienced pianists sometimes do this and youngsters who are struggling with the notes certainly need extra guidance to keep the whole phrase structure in mind.

PEDALLING

Teachers will find some pedalling marked in early grade pieces but *legato* pedalling is not really required until around Grades 4 or 5. Pupils are often fascinated with the effect of using the sustaining pedal and finding the right places in early grades to begin to use this skill is an opportunity not to be missed. The co-ordination of foot and hands in *legato* pedalling usually takes longer to acquire but is necessary for much of the piano repertoire beyond Grade 4. It is important to keep the heel on the floor when pedalling, using only the toes and front sole of the foot, rather than the whole leg, which causes tension in the muscles. When pedalling becomes natural, it can be safely put on 'auto pilot', providing the pupil is always listening carefully to avoid over-generous pedalling with a blurred result.

EDITIONS

There is often concern about editorial suggestions in early music and the realization of ornaments. In the early grades the editor has followed markings given by the composer and sometimes added further articulation marks or dynamics, in keeping with the style and period. The footnotes give details of which marks are the composer's and which are editorial. At the higher grades there are fewer marks on the music itself but the footnotes give suggestions for phrasing and articulation. When the dynamics are only editorial suggestions, they do not have to be slavishly followed. All music needs dynamic colour and the use of this is purely subjective. Phrasing will inevitably cause dynamic fluctuations, apart from the higher or lower levels of sound that may be chosen for a longer section. In the more contemporary pieces, the musical markings are usually the composer's and should be incorporated into the performance for an authentic account.

ORNAMENTS

The Associated Board prints the following advice to teachers:

> Where appropriate, pieces have been checked with original source material and edited as necessary for instructional purposes. Fingering, phrasing, bowing, metronome marks and the editorial realization of ornaments (where given) are for guidance but are not comprehensive or obligatory.

Ornaments are just another aspect of the performance. If it is possible for them to be incorporated comfortably into the rhythm of the piece, they are always welcome as an additional aspect of the style. If playing the suggested ornament is going to upset the pulse, then it is much better to shorten the ornament into a turn or mordent, or to leave it out entirely to keep the structure of the piece intact. It is at Grade 6 that pieces really requiring ornamentation should only be chosen when the ornaments can be incorporated, even if in modified form. In the lower grades examiners are happy to accept performances without ornaments, providing that other musical aspects, such as phrasing and dynamics, have been given consideration.

THE SUPPORTING TESTS

Scales – Key sense and agility are both developed gradually with the requirements throughout the grades. An even, rhythmic finger touch with smoothly incorporated thumb turns is a vital technical basis. Arpeggios help pupils to become much more familiar with the extent of the keyboard and also develop chord awareness. Keeping elbows a little away from the sides avoids the bumps and sudden lurches that sometimes get in the way of a fluent progression though the octaves. Co-ordination is essential and, as in everything else, an inner rhythm needs to underpin these technical requirements. Contrary scales also help independence of hands. Different rhythmic patterns, dynamics and forms of articulation all add to the pianist's control of tone, which is the musical equivalent of an artist's palette of colours.

Sight-reading – The examiner will give the candidate 30 seconds to try out and look carefully through the sight-reading test. Many candidates are too shy to actually play parts of the test but this is strongly to be encouraged, to give confidence to the attempt. The first essential is to set up a basic rhythm and to count out the structure of the first bar or so in order to give the time-values real meaning. The time-honoured words 'Keep going' still apply and pupils should learn to ignore notation mistakes and press on in their chosen tempo, regardless of accidents along the way. Examiners consider key sense and rhythm equally and appreciate courageous attempts to keep the piece in shape. So often candidates will falter or stop when a mistake occurs which could easily be overcome with a different approach. The eventual value of adequate sight-reading far outweighs the difficulties of acquiring it in the early stages.

Aural tests – These days teachers are frequently including aural tests during the course of a lesson, using phrases to be sung or clapped that are met in the pieces. The various skills that are developed by these tests help an all-round awareness of music, and the D test, recognizing various aspects of a short piece played by the examiner, is particularly valuable for mature listening and appreciation. Many candidates and teachers worry about the singing tests but it is recognition of pitch and intervals that is being assessed, not vocal quality. Humming, singing an octave lower or whistling are perfectly acceptable ways of responding. The C test in lower grades can be answered by clapping or singing the change, putting up a hand when the difference happens or explaining it in simple terms. It is not necessary to give exact rhythm or pitch changes; the usual answers are in this style, 'It went faster after the first note' or 'The last-but-one note was lower'.

Teachers with limited piano skills often use recordings to help with the last test; sometimes the examples can be put on tape by a helpful colleague. The current aural tests are producing higher marks than the previous set and most pupils can manage at least some parts. Examiners assess the response as a whole, so if one test is a regular problem, it is only a small part of this section and should not be allowed to become out of proportion in the pupil's mind.

Finally, here are a few general observations which have proved their worth over the years:

- In order to have a clear idea of what examiners are looking for, refer to the Board's Basis of Assessment, which is printed in *These Music Exams*. This gives a guide as to how examiners award marks for the pieces and which elements in the playing contribute to the different categories: Pass, Merit and Distinction.
- All the sections of the exam are individually assessed positively or negatively from the Pass mark. Marks are not added from zero or deducted from the total.
- Careful selection of the pieces makes all the difference to the preparation period. This is now much easier with the increased choice in the new lists.
- Aim to be ready for the exam a few weeks before the expected date. Gradual preparation is essential for reliability on the Big Day.
- Incorporate scales, sight-reading and aural in small doses in most lessons, extracting suitable material from current pieces as well as using the specimen tests.
- A positive attitude to nerves and realistic hopes will create a more helpful climate than over-optimistic expectations. All candidates feel a degree of nervousness and examiners understand this natural response. They will assess the playing on the day with accuracy, giving detailed comments on what occurs, but will also be alert to signs of musicality and achievement which still show despite anxious slips or hesitations.
- Playing to friends and parents builds confidence and this performance practice helps to make the point that musicians, even professionals, rarely live up to their own expectations. It is the effort that goes into the attempt which counts at all levels and foothills are essential on the way to greater heights.

GRADE 1

The first exam is potentially an exciting event and the choice of pieces is crucial, as pupils will probably be living with the programme for longer than any previous repertoire. In the early grades, basic accuracy of notes and time at a suitable tempo will achieve a Pass. More musical interest and character in the piece will attract Merit marks, but really polished playing will be needed for a Distinction. Serious errors will, of course, lower the category of the marks but examiners are well aware of the human element and balance the positive and negative qualities of the whole performance rather than focusing on any isolated aspect. You will find further information in the Basis of Assessment printed in *These Music Exams*.

LIST A

Candidates often play the List A piece first in their programme, so choose one of the items that is well within the technical comfort zone. A1 and A2 both have appealing, strong melodies. A2 is perhaps the easier in terms of notes, but watch the co-ordination from bar 9 onwards. A5 will also suit pupils with a little less technical confidence, but those with good finger control will succeed well with A6, which also needs subtlety of balance and phrasing. All the List A pieces depend upon clarity of articulation and an emerging sense of phrasing, and these are the first things the examiners look for beyond a safe coverage of notes and time.

LIST B

All these pieces help to develop a sense of expression and a *legato* touch. B4 is very straightforward, but needs a pupil who will take the time to play a simple melody musically. B1 will come across rather like a piece from List A, so the balance of the overall programme needs to be kept in mind. B2, B3 and B6 will suit musical pupils with an ability to shape a melody, and B5 is ideal for reluctant readers of the bass, but requires good co-ordination.

LIST C

There is a wide range of different idioms in these choices, and although the jazzy items are always immensely popular, they do have some quite demanding rhythmic aspects. C4 needs quite a broad range of dynamics, and some musical sensitivity. Lively, energetic pupils will go for C5 and C6, and of course the jazzers will enjoy C2. C3 will suit those who find a good *legato* difficult, but who have quite well-developed co-ordination. Above all, the pieces chosen from List C should come across with a completely different atmosphere from those chosen from Lists A and B.

A:1 Handel *Minuet*

Children always enjoy pieces with a strong rhythm and melody. This minuet has both – with the extra benefit of cheerful dance music written in a familiar Grade 1 key.

The vitality of the pulse depends on a well-marked (but not too heavy) first beat, and lighter second and third crotchets in every bar. Phrases fall into comfortable four-bar sections, with the main points given gentle emphasis. This happens first on the B of bar 4, and recurs throughout, given the correct elegant shaping.

Examiners will appreciate a smoothly graded *crescendo* from bar 17 to the final *forte*, as well as a clear difference at bar 9, which is the first chance to show real contrast. Fingering, as always, is a matter of convenience, providing the musical effect is convincing, but the printed fingering from bar 19 is likely to be the safest approach.

The little slurs are there just to suggest particular *legato* corners – don't make too much of an issue of them at this early stage. The bass crotchets are stylish if lightly detached, and this combines practicality with musicality, as it's much easier that way, especially when the left hand spans larger intervals. There are no hidden perils and the piece will be a happy introduction to the syllabus.

A:2 Hook *Gavotta in C*

The key to the musical door of this little piece is its two-in-a-bar dance rhythm, turning a simple collection of notes into a charming miniature. Without this awareness it could plod along rather boringly, especially if all crotchets are given the same weight. Not many pupils can give the ideal musical subtlety, so help them to go for a lively tempo, showing the four-bar phrasing with its 'feminine endings' (leaning on the penultimate beat such as the first D of bar 4), and making the dynamics at bars 9 and 11 a real contrast.

A very slow tempo would drain the life out of the music, as would slowing up for the quavers. A lot of candidates will probably cut short the minim at bar 8 in a rush to get on to the next bar.

There is one challenge to co-ordination at bars 9–10. This could turn into a frequent stumbling-block in exams, unless the physical memory is firmly in place, with sensible fingering part of the learning process.

Examiners always appreciate quick recovery from slips, so if an accident does happen, the pupil should go straight on to the next bar, keeping the rhythm going, which is worth more marks than, 'Can I start again please?'.

A:3 Türk *There it goes at full gallop*

'Full gallop' describes the effect of nerves on many candidates. It is so easy to rush under pressure, and a piece that may have been polished at the last lesson can fall at the first fence in the exam.

This piece is quite demanding in its finger patterns and also in the amount of musical detail. Slow practice, with fingering and slurs included from the start, will form a safe foundation. The tempo indication is lively, and the gallop is a one-in-a-bar controlled rhythm, not a mad rush. The upbeats should be light, and could be detached if you like the effect. Quick thinking is necessary to change dynamic in faster-moving pieces, so help your students to think ahead in their performance practice. The two little mordents are not difficult to include, or acciaccaturas would also work, but play for safety, and leave them out if they cause any slowing of the tempo.

The crotchet at bar 8 might be held too long, unless the player really feels the basic beat continuously, but the final pause is a good chance to catch the breath before the next piece.

A:4 J. C. F. Bach *Menuet in C*

This minuet comes from a collection comprising some of the first keyboard pieces to be composed for the early piano. It is both charming and elegant and the dancers definitely have smiles on their faces.

The C major key signature will fill many pupils with glee, but the lack of accidentals or a key signature doesn't necessarily mean 'easy'. In fact the piece demands a developing variety of touch to lighten and shape the upbeats, giving the dance its buoyancy. In bar 3, for instance, lightly detaching the final four right-hand quavers would be very effective and will help the left-hand phrasing as it will want to instinctively shorten the upbeat. Indeed, it is often a good idea to match right-hand and left-hand movements throughout at this early stage, even where this means allowing the left hand to play *legato*. Choreographing both hands together eases many co-ordination problems that may otherwise occur.

Watch out for the almost inevitable but unwanted pauses at the end of the first four bars and at the first double bar. The editorial commas imply a 'breath', not the 'full stop' which can characterize so many early-grade performances; hands need to get ready quickly and eyes to travel fluently to the beginning of the next line and moments like this are often better memorized.

Finally, keep the left hand a fraction lighter than the right. Even at this grade a sense of balance between the hands is worth cultivating and will make an enormous difference to the effectiveness of the performance.

A:5 W. F. Bach *Air in A minor*

If your pupil is of a more melancholy disposition then this haunting yet very beautiful air is for them. It will suit the less confident performer because there are few changes of hand position and the suggested *legato* line not only enhances the character but also allows the fingers to stay in contact with the keys throughout.

The melody will need some sensitive dynamic shaping and mustn't be too rhythmically rigid. The pupil will need to be particularly careful in bar 4 and in the second-time bar, where there is a risk of an accent on the fourth quaver beat. This is also a classic moment for miscounting and a late, scrambled entry. If all else fails then repeat the C on the second crotchet beat until the rhythm is secure and unhurried.

It is well worth pointing out how the wonderful major/minor contrast in this piece can be used as a springboard for dynamic contrast and change of tonal colour, without which the piece could become a little dull. A little extra guidance may be needed with the left hand in bars 9–12 to familiarize the pupil with the wandering hand position and accidentals.

A small *ritenuto* will enhance the end, and it is worth insisting on the left-hand fingering in the final bar which, though unusual, works well.

A:6 Mouret *La Montagnarde*

If the French title doesn't convince you that this is the dance of a Scottish 'Highland girl', then the bagpipe drone effect in the left hand may well do so. Unfortunately, the enjoyment of playing the open fifths, coupled with the *forte* dynamic, could easily result in a little too much enthusiasm and the risk of the piece becoming bottom heavy. The chords need to be kept light and the grace note gently tucked in, indeed almost played with the D, and the melody then allowed to skip its way over the top.

Otherwise, the first two lines are reassuringly straightforward, and if your pupil can play with a light, crisp *staccato* and buoyant, confident phrasing then there is little to trouble them until line 3. Here, life becomes a touch less comfortable; the left hand has a risky leap up to an F sharp and the right hand needs to move from its by now too familiar position for the D major scale in bar 10. Ideally, the left hand needs to get ready immediately the right hand plays its G at the beginning of line 3, and working at this will pay enormous dividends under the pressure of an exam. Hands only too often lose their way at moments such as these.

Make the most of the varied dynamics and allow the pupil the luxury of a flamboyant Highland fling at the end.

B:1 Beethoven *Air from Little Russia*

A theme used for variations needs a strong individuality to give continuity and to keep its own voice despite the various disguises on the way.

The dotted rhythms deserve careful attention, and could suffer from being too slow, almost turning into 6/8 time, or too crisp, almost double dotted. The first scenario is the usual problem, and the latter does happen but is more musically acceptable.

An improvised duet can also add enormous fun to the lesson. With the pupil playing one hand and teacher playing the other, it is possible to consider the left-hand *legato* and phrasing, plus the small slurs in the right hand, as only one hand has to be managed. Swapping around changes the focal points, and the final solo version is likely to be much more polished.

The finger changing in bars 9 and 10 is not necessary. It is easier to use 4-4-3-3-2-2, then change to 3 in bar 11, especially when coping with those essential dots. Keeping a light finger attack will help the repeated notes to speak crisply, and will keep the piece from becoming too strident at the loud moments.

Crotchet =120 is plenty fast enough, and it dances along like a children's song, rhythmically strong but still light-hearted.

B:2 Grechaninov *Lament*

Although children may like sad music, they often find it difficult to control the speed, getting faster and faster as the notes become more secure.

Examiners are familiar with the 'express train' approach, when notes are safe but the tempo is far too fast for the spirit of the piece to survive. Try walking around the room with the pupil, both of you humming the melody, putting your feet down in a measured minim pattern. When the physical actions are set with the music, the tempo memory will probably be in place for the playing.

Aim for a really connected warm-toned *legato*. Against this, the left hand gently puts in the offbeat crotchets, just detached, not too *staccato*, and always lifted for the rests, which are important throughout.

The middle section, bars 9–13, gives a contrast of texture which makes a surprisingly strong impact. Both hands play *legato*, and shape the slurs together.

Quite a lot of instructions are printed in bars 12 and 13, giving a chance to make the climax of the piece really expressive. The second pause, in bar 13, is longer than the first, but the quiet echo should not linger too long before the main theme returns. Demonstration by the teacher is often worth hundreds of descriptive words, especially in the more subtle pieces.

B:3 d'Indy *La Pernette*

The footnote tells the real drama of the French girl in the title, at her spinning wheel on the morning her lover is to be hanged. This grisly tale may well appeal to some pupils, but others will need to be guided towards the more musical possibilities and general mood. Spinning wheels may need some explanation in these days of high technology.

The left hand suggests the wheel, and we hope it will be a well-oiled, smoothly flowing action. Lots of left-hand practice will be needed as the notes must be on 'auto-pilot' before they can reliably provide a gentle background.

Balance is a word that will appear on many mark forms when this piece is played. The left hand is demanding, but must always be quieter than the right-hand melody, which needs musical phrasing and smooth grading of tone. It would be a pity to overlook the quaver rests in bars 2 and 3 – think of them perhaps as little sobs, as the poor girl sings.

The phrase beginning on D in bar 5 could be more positive in sound than the opening, then gradually drop down towards bar 9. The final *crescendo* is not thunderous, always warm, and peaks with the left-hand chords. Make sure these can be found without any anxious searching, and if the octaves are too much for small hands, leave out the top note of each.

B:4 Anon. *Morning has broken*

This is an effective and simple arrangement of a traditional tune. Very well written for small hands, it will be deservedly popular not only with young pupils wanting to sing the well-known words, but also with adult beginners fondly remembering their school assemblies.

The morning may break but the *legato* must not, and herein lies the main difficulty: giving the song a sense of line and vocal shape. Be particularly careful of the first bar; pupils will want to hold on to the left-hand C but it needs to be released once the right hand has played its E, and then got ready for the left-hand entry in bar 2. Elsewhere, encourage a smooth overlapping between the notes, and delicate shading at the ends of phrases, lightening the hand. A musical pupil will instinctively soften the right-hand D in bar 18 for instance, matching the decaying left-hand chord and finally lifting the hands together in order to 'breathe' before the next phrase.

The suggested fingering is excellent and will help avoid hesitations, but it is not always the most obvious finger that goes down (bar 5 for instance) so careful learning will be necessary. It is possibly a good idea to practise some of these moments with your pupil before leaving them to their own devices.

Note the 'Not too fast' indication. A pupil launching in nervously at an unsuitably quick speed could so easily spoil a well-prepared and musical performance. Encourage them to sing the final line of the tune to themselves before starting, both to calm nerves and to set an effective tempo.

B:5 A. E. Müller *The Cuckoo Waltz*

Just the piece for the Spring session of exams; the title really tells all. It is a charming and attractive waltz and an excellent piece for reluctant readers of the bass clef.

It needs a light, articulated touch throughout the 'cuckoos', and a gentle, elegant left-hand arpeggiated accompaniment. Interpret the left-hand phrasing musically – the final crotchet of each bar shouldn't be articulated too severely – and encourage a subtle *decrescendo* towards the end of each bar. It could almost be played *legato* across the bar as long as it has musical shape.

Good co-ordination will be needed at times, particularly where the *staccato* right hand contrasts the *legato* left hand. Some slow practice will reap rewards here, just as it will with the couplet chords in the left hand and subsequently the right hand towards the end. The wrist needs to 'give' slightly on the first chord and rise on the lighter second chord. So many pupils seem to reverse this movement and it can hinder natural phrasing.

The dynamics need subtle variety. The two cuckoos in the opening, one more distant than the other, will require good tonal control and light upbeats. The main melody which follows must be well projected above the accompaniment and the wrist of the left hand should be supple and flexible to avoid a wooden tone.

A gentle *ritenuto* will signal the return of the cuckoos in bar 21. Encourage the pupils to keep the hands still for the crotchet rest at the end of the piece as the evening arrives and the birds cease their song.

B:6 Fritz Spindler *Song without Words*

The wonderful thing about songs without words is that you can shamelessly put words to the tune, and with young pupils this will give you lots of scope for discussing phrasing, breathing and dynamic shape as well as character. Practising playing the left hand whilst singing the tune is invaluable ear-training and will help to learn the piece, but in this instance you may need to confine yourself to the first line, as the top 'A' will prove too stratospheric for most pupils.

It may be worth approaching the last line first as the offbeat left hand may cause a few anxious moments. It helps to think of the left-hand quavers as leading into the next melody note rather than following on from the previous one.

There are other general concerns though. The left-hand accompaniment has all the inherent dangers of an Alberti bass, in particular that it may become too strident. The pupil will need to cultivate a light thumb and avoid detaching the final note of each bar too severely.

The melody needs to sing through, so slightly more weight behind the fingers is needed, but keep the grace note light in bar 14. It would be a good idea to encourage the pupil to listen to the *ends* of the notes so that they can grade the attack on the following note; this will help grade the dynamic shape and avoid a 'bump' on the first note after the tie (bars 3–4 and 29–30).

There is a slightly melancholy character to this piece so the tempo should not be too fast, although it needs to be one-in-a-bar. Explore the possibility of a slight *ritenuto* at the end and hold the final note for its full length to allow it a natural *decrescendo*.

C:1 Carol Barratt *Susy, Little Susy*

It is best to sort out the first few bars before the pupil begins work alone. 'What's the first note?' and 'My hands are bumping into each other', are predictable reactions, but soon resolved. The left hand goes over the top, and should give the right hand enough room. Meanwhile, the right-hand melody sings away in popular folk style, giving lots of shape to the phrases and grading the dynamics evenly.

The rhythm of bar 3 could be tricky, but less of a problem if the counting has started right from the first silent beat of the piece. After bar 10, the left hand moves down the piano, and the second half of the piece is easier to assemble.

One hand *legato*, the other *staccato* also needs an independent physical memory, and may take a few weeks to settle reliably. Some setbacks are to be expected, but patience and encouragement will win out in most cases.

Bars 17–18 are the most musically telling in a performance. It will be a pleasure to hear candidates showing the *diminuendo* to the left-hand E flat thoughtfully, then judging the last rest and placing of the final chord, rather reminiscent of the traditional organ grinder, who might well have been part of this happy scene.

C:2 Laurie Holloway *Walking fingers*

'It don't mean a thing if it ain't got that swing' introduced the Associated Board's new Jazz syllabus, and many jazzers probably take it for granted that these fingers are 'swinging' while they walk. Pupils often have a natural feel for jazz rhythms, and should take to the idiom without difficulty. This is not the right place for a full explanation of swung rhythm, but for those who are not quite certain, imagine the piece played in 12/8 time, not 4/4, and you have made a good start. The left-hand minims are played exactly as written, while the right hand makes the most of the anticipation – the tied notes in bars 2, 4 and 6 – also an unmistakable jazz characteristic. A 'straight' account, played as printed, will be worth just as many marks – it's up to you to choose your approach.

Many pupils will tend to rush the half bars where both hands are playing minims. A large reminder on the page often helps, but the right 'feel' is even better.

After a positive but not aggressive opening phrase, it would be fun to make a *diminuendo* to bar 5, where the third phrase begins. After this, choose whether to go for a bold ending or a more laid-back treatment of the last chords.

C:3 Shostakovich *March*

This is an old favourite, conjuring up images of marching toy soldiers and comic antics, and will suit a pupil with an unreliable *legato* as the melody is most effective when the crotchets are detached. It has a deceptively easy opening but should probably be avoided by slow readers unless they have an excellent physical memory. The numerous accidentals and slightly unpredictable lie of notes in bars 9–16 and the final four bars may cause some anxiety.

The dynamics enhance the humour of the piece so make the most of them. Don't start too loudly: save the more robust tone for the 'trumpets' when they enter in bar 9, followed by a less sure-footed *piano* as the rather undisciplined military band loses its place in the music. It begins afresh (*forte*) – but the same thing happens, so the march continues.

There may be some co-ordination problems in the final four bars, as the left hand takes up the opening motif. Consistency of fingering will be vital here to help the physical memory. If this is not secure then the pupil will be forced to read the notes and this may result in some hesitancy under the pressure of an exam.

The tempo should be steady and not too fast (minim = 84 is given), and make sure the final performance has a sense of humour; good, clear articulation will help, as will a smile on the face!

C:4 Jean-Marc Allerme *C'est lui qui a commencé*

A haunting, unusual piece – and not just in terms of the title ('It's he who began'). The phrase lengths have a wonderful irregularity, most are three bars long but one is five bars long, and this gives the piece a timelessness and improvisatory feel that will appeal to the more musically responsive pupil. The soulful melody sings a sad song over a 'sighing' chromatic left hand.

There are a lot of questions posed by the absence of dynamic markings (just the *mezzo forte* at the beginning). It is vital, of course, that there *is* dynamic interest and that *mezzo forte* is treated as a dynamic range and used to give the melody musical shape. The dynamics could, for instance, follow the rise and fall of the pitch. The more major-sounding middle section might be *forte* in order to highlight a more optimistic thought, but then *mezzo forte* again as the spirits wane and the sad thoughts return.

Point out the left-hand melody in the final six bars to your pupil and help them to develop the important technique of balancing the hands the other way around.

Encourage the pupil to 'breathe' gently between phrases and make sure that they give full value to the semibreves in bar 14. Listening intently to the decay of the note can often help prevent panicked counting.

Finally, let them hold the final note as long as they dare to sustain the atmosphere.

C:5 Philip Cannon *Mighty Mohican*

Whilst this is sure to appeal to many, be on your guard. The 'Stamp it out mighty fierce' indication may be a 'red rag to a bull' (or buffalo) in the hands of the more boisterous pupil. This is clearly a perfect piece for the aspiring Indian warriors amongst your pupils, but do point out to them that this Mohican needs just a little domesticity if the piece is not to sound too much like a wild, undisciplined noise.

It is worth noting that there *are* some dynamics and they are not all *molto fortissimo*. The opening is only *forte*, so the big noise needs to be saved for later. It will be particularly important for the dynamic to drop significantly in bars 8 and 18 to show the *crescendo*.

A whole bar's rest is always a worrying time for the teacher (and examiner). Few pupils will give the full length, so be quite firm about counting bars 10 and 20. Fortunately, the words 'mighty Mohican' fit rather well in these bars (to the opening rhythm) and, if said in the pupil's head, will hopefully avoid too many premature entries.

Other than this, and providing the phrasing and rests are observed, the piece fairly much plays itself. There is one slightly unusual but effective fingering in bar 22 (right hand) and notice that the piece does not finish until after the final two-beat rest – so hands remain still to enhance the drama.

C:6 Milhaud *Elma Joue*

Physical dexterity does not always go hand in hand with musicality, and here is a chance for the nimble fingered to show off with justifiable pride, perhaps leaving their more emotionally expressive contemporaries to linger over the slower choices.

The tempo is a lively two-in-a-bar, but not a headlong rush. Teachers will see at a glance that success depends on bars 5 and 6, 14 and 15; there should be no slowing up here, but a lovely even stream of semiquavers making a gradual *diminuendo* the first time, then an exciting *crescendo* later. The notes are not difficult to learn despite the stratospheric start on that high F. It's all in the fingering and management of the scale, which turns out to be C major, beginning in an unusual place.

A firm *legato* is needed from bar 10, with a good, long-lasting tied C in the bass. The changing time signature in bar 9 is no problem – just play what's there and it makes sense, easily switching back to 2/4 for the final section.

Avoid a stomach-churning end to this piece by using the rest to get into position, leaving out the lower right-hand C if necessary. This is a high-risk piece, but great fun. Play for safety, and give it to those with lots of confidence.

GRADE 2

For those who have previously taken Grade 1, this experience of an exam will add insight to the selection of the pieces for the next grade. Teachers will remember which items were a particular success and will be able to select something similar for the next attempt. There is a great variety of choice within these lists and it would be good experience for your pupil to have three pieces in very different styles and moods in order to explore a wide span of expression.

LIST A

Do have a look at the alternative pieces not printed in the album before making final choices. A1 and A5 are uncomplicated, though not simple. They would both suit pupils with a sunny disposition. A2 and A6 will need more technically accomplished pianists; A3 may be a little risky for a nervous pupil, with its left-hand leaps. The ability to phrase convincingly and give some dynamic variety will be welcome in all performances.

LIST B

B1 needs a lightness of touch and sensitivity to shape. B2 and B3 will work best for imaginative pupils who can shape musically. B2 has a few tricky moments. The well-known Schumann, B6, has instant melodic appeal, but a few challenges in balance and co-ordination. All these expressive pieces give opportunities for a developing sense of *rubato* to add musical conviction.

LIST C

C1 is ideal for sensitive pupils with good tonal control, as is C6, where matching of tone is so important. C2 will suit those with a sense of humour and secure rhythm. There are otherwise few problems, but it does need character. C3 is right into the reggae groove, underpinned with a very firm sense of pulse. This will be a popular choice. Both C4 and C5 give opportunities for vivid, imaginative playing, with a secure, regular beat. To really catch the mood of each of these pieces, tempo should be quite an important consideration.

A:1 Attwood *Allegro*

If your pupils are a little reluctant to practise their scales then here is a cunning way of introducing them 'through the back door'. This is cheerful music suiting pupils with a sunny disposition. It is fairly uncomplicated in character, but less straightforward in reality, despite its C major key signature, ABA structure and not a black note in sight! The all-too-familiar ingredients of a light, even Alberti bass coupled with a scalic melody are there, and they are often the recipe for a dull, strident performance.

The secret is balance. The left hand (and particularly left thumb) needs to be kept very light and unobtrusive. It will help the pupil if they weight the hand to the outside, and this can be encouraged by some practice in holding down the bottom note and keeping the following three *pianissimo*, with the fingers close to the keys. By contrast, the right hand needs a brighter tone; more rounded fingers and a slightly higher finger action will help. Once the right balance is achieved the music will respond to plenty of melodic shape; the suggested dynamics work particularly well.

The suggested tempo marking is very effective; the piece mustn't be too fast as it will lose some of its charm. Equally, some sprightly phrasing will add to the good humour. Treat the slurs as bowing marks since this should avoid too many hiccups and disjointed phrases, particularly in the opening, bars 10–12 and similar places.

With a free, easy technique this is an entrancing and effective piece.

A:2 Beethoven *Ecossaise in E flat*

The quick and energetic écossaise rivalled the minuet in popularity during the first part of the 19th century and this short, lively example of the dance will present few problems note-wise. In the wrong hands, however, it could lose much of its buoyancy and humour.

The secret to playing this piece successfully and drawing out the dance character is 'in the wrist' as they say. The right hand needs a relaxed 'bounce' for the *staccato* quavers and the wrist must 'give' on all the crotchets to avoid a too-harsh *sforzando*. Remember that this marking in Beethoven's music does not have the same meaning as in Prokofiev's, for example, and is merely a slight emphasis.

In bars 5 and 6 the right-hand wrist needs to give on the first of the quavers and rise through the bar to enable a short second quaver and light, *staccato* quavers at the end of the bar. With a little lateral movement as well, the phrasing then becomes easy and effortless.

The left-hand wrist needs equal consideration. Allowing it to relax on the first chord of each bar and rise for the second will help lighten the final crotchet. Avoid making the second beats too short though. As with the *sforzando*, this phrase marking needs to be interpreted and should not be too abrupt.

Note that the repeats are not required in the exam and observe the dynamics carefully. For the right pupil this piece should prove a good confidence booster as it responds well to a positive touch and there are no worrying jumps.

A:3 Telemann *Gigue à l'Angloise*

The gigue was the most popular of all Baroque instrumental dances and this, like most of them, is burlesque in style and needs a sense of humour.

Setting the tempo may well prove the downfall of some performances: too fast and fingers could easily lose direction. The two-semiquaver anacrusis is also likely to trip up a slightly nervous pupil so it would be valuable to count in at least two bars and practise controlling the fingers here.

Remember that the suggested phrasing is essentially bowing markings. Don't complicate matters by insisting that pupils detach the final semiquaver of the opening or second quaver of each three-quaver group for instance. Instead, enhance the dance character by using subtle dynamic shading, lightening the hand for the final two quavers of each group and insisting that the second group of each bar is lighter to avoid too many 'first beats'.

There are some slightly concerning leaps in the left hand, which will need attention. A glance at the hand at these points will prove invaluable for security and will be vital in bar 10, where the left hand has to jump two octaves. Don't rely on the eyes though – here is a chance to practise 'blindfold', memorizing the distance the hand has to travel.

Try to detach the final three quavers of each half, and keep on the ends of the fingers throughout to give a bright, exciting edge to the tone.

A:4 Clarke *Aire in C*

Few teachers own a harpsichord, but it's usually possible to play a short recorded item to the pupil, giving them the idea of the original sound of this kind of music.

The tempo and ornaments must be considered in relation to each other. A brisk tempo, as indicated, is stylish and invigorating, but puts the printed decorations out of reach for some Grade 2 players. Simple triplets followed by the dotted-quaver–semiquaver patterns in small print work just as well at bars 7 and 15.

A slightly slower tempo could work, providing the rhythm still feels like two beats, but the omission of ornaments would be more obvious, putting greater responsibility on the phrasing and dynamic plan. The articulation suggested in the footnotes certainly adds to the style, but may be too complicated for some candidates – a *legato* version is quite acceptable in exams. Make the most of the change of key from bar 9; a quieter start would be welcome, but otherwise the dynamics naturally rise and fall with the pitch.

Some left-hand practice will be needed for the held minims and the two-part writing around bars 10 and 11. Throughout the piece, the upbeat quavers should sound as if they are leading to the next main beat – the beginnings of thinking 'forward' rather than vertically perhaps?

A:5 Mozart *Menuett in G*

Many hundreds of minuets have been played in exams without the candidates knowing what the word means. Dance music is not enough to go on with today's gymnastic rock and pop as the norm, so a lively description will help – with actions perhaps?

The tempo indication may be on the fast side for the average candidate, but always aim for a good first beat, with much lighter second and third crotchets. The slurs give character and grace; just lift the last notes lightly as a real *staccato* would be intrusive.

The left-hand rests are important, adding rhythmic point, and fingering will need some careful investigation. The printed suggestions in bars 1–3 work well, but pupils may feel more comfortable beginning with thumbs in both hands, then, in the left hand, using 1-2-3, 1-2-3, 4-2-1, 2. Whatever you decide, the same applies for bars 13–16. Safety wins over artistic ideals, and thumb on the E in bar 17 will avoid hesitation at this slightly dangerous moment.

Ornaments, providing they are within the rhythm, will add extra polish, but triplets at bars 4 and 19 would also be fine.

Try making a *crescendo* in bar 6 to the double bar, then beginning at bar 9 at a quieter level. Returning to a warmer dynamic for the final two phrases will round the piece off nicely.

A:6 Oxinaga *Minué in F*

Joaquín Oxinaga was a priest and organist in the first half of the 18th century, and this piece comes from a selection of Basque music of the period. It was likely to have been originally played on the organ, and you will probably hear the influence of Haydn.

Even management of the triplets is vital; they could easily become semiquaver–semiquaver–quaver. It's a good plan for pupils to practise without the suggested decoration, then decide which to include without upsetting the even flow. The appoggiaturas at bars 4, 8, 10, 12 and 16 might all become half or two-thirds the value of the following beat as printed, which is just as easy to play as the plain version. The acciaccaturas are more taxing; play them with a small light action. The triplets in bars 2 and 14 could be deftly slipped in, or omitted. Ornaments sometimes obscure the main points of phrasing if they are not comfortably achieved. Don't miss the feminine endings underneath at bars 4, 8 and 12, and, of course, in the final bars – the most emphatic of all.

'Amiable' is a pleasant instruction at the start. A warm tone is enjoyable here, and the little G minor passage, bars 9 and 10, is an opportunity to find a different colour before coming out into the Spanish sunshine again for the last section.

B:1 J.-B. Duvernoy *Study in F*

Don't let the title dissuade you from considering this piece – it is an entrancing waltz, evoking images of whirling dancers, and it deserves a hearing. Indeed, before playing it to a pupil, why not suggest a more appropriate title.

This said, this is not a piece for the heavy-handed. It requires a controlled lightness of touch, particularly in the left hand, and will suit the budding ballerinas amongst your pupils but not the rugby players.

To capture the elegance and charm it will be helpful to work at the 'choreography' of the hands. The right hand, in particular, will benefit from a relaxed drop on the first beat of each bar, allowing the wrist to rise through the final quavers and lighten the tone. There should be no violent emphasis on the 'hat' accents or snatched *staccato* notes to disturb the naive simplicity.

The left hand needs to complement this by slightly more tone on the first beat of each bar and then a *decrescendo* through the two chords. The *staccato* is achieved from the surface of the key and is more a finger action than a wrist action, the latter being too heavy a touch.

Encourage a slight *ritenuto* in bars 8 and 24 (not forgetting to play the *da capo*); this will 'ease in' the melody and grade the dynamics carefully so that the tone does not become too robust in the *forte* bars.

B:2 Gedike *Night in the Woods*

This is wonderful, pictorial piano writing. An excellent title conjures up images of a cold, lonely and rather frightening stay in a Russian wood – full of strange noises and unexpected happenings.

There is so much drama in this short piece but the effectiveness of the performance will depend upon the widest range of dynamic and phrasing to portray the story. Take all of Gedike's markings at face value and show all of the rests clearly.

Technically, the piece may pose a few problems for a pupil who hasn't yet developed a range of touch and articulation. The first six notes alone require couplet phrasing, finger *staccato* and a full-length crotchet at the end. The wrist action will be all-important here: lift for the second note, keep the hand light for the *staccato* quavers and drop gently on the *tenuto* crotchet.

Try an alternative to the given fingering on the last beat of bar 6 by putting the third finger in each hand on the Cs, jumping to fifth finger in the right hand and thumb in the left hand. Bars 13 and onwards are a typical moment for hesitation and uncertainty of notes, particularly in an exam. Make sure the pupil uses the rests to prepare the hand and can 'measure' the distance without looking at the keyboard. Bars 16–19 have a 'what's coming next?' character and a small *ritenuto* in bar 19 wouldn't come amiss. The listener shouldn't be kept in suspense too long, however, so hands should be ready for the next phrase early, even if they don't actually play as soon as they arrive.

Make a feature of the F major chord in bar 26 and lift the final chords together as if playing with one hand. Small hands can just play the top A of the left-hand octave.

B:3 Guilmant *Child's Song*

This is a well-known teaching piece which needs little introduction. It is rightly popular, being beautiful, expressive and an excellent introduction to *cantabile* playing. It will suit a musical pianist who will naturally shape the vocal line.

The piece looks quite busy on the page, so a pupil may need some reassurance once they have seen it. In fact, providing the pupil is a reasonably fluent reader, the piece shouldn't pose too many problems but it will certainly prove more challenging for those pupils who tend to read slowly and commit the notes to memory.

There are a few unexpected twists and turns harmonically which will need some guidance in the early stages, as the notes do not fall naturally under the fingers. The written fingering is certainly useful but not necessarily the only option and some flexibility might be needed. Changing the finger on the repeated Cs in the opening and elsewhere may help enhance the phrasing but be too fussy for some pupils. You might allow two 'second' fingers here, beginning with the fifth finger on the first note.

Musically, the piece needs a natural fluency, so try a gentle two-in-a-bar (not four) and keep the left-hand accompaniment light and unobtrusive. Slightly 'flatter' fingers will help achieve the right sound. Encourage a slight 'breath' at the ends of phrases, but 'interpret' the phrase markings rather than taking them too literally since an abrupt *staccato*, or a 'snatching' of the final notes, will not enhance the character.

You may feel that the tempo marking is somewhat on the fast side, in which case allow the piece to be taken at a more relaxed speed. Remember, however, that the slower the piece is taken, the greater the amount of control needed to give the melody dynamic shape.

B:4 C. Gurlitt *Moderato*

Tranquillo is a word that does not easily spring to mind in an exam or when starting to learn a new piece. A gentle walking pace gives space for the four-bar phrases to make their point, and a couple of deep breaths before beginning could help to settle the mood. Classical feminine endings are an important part of the phrasing, needing gentle emphasis on the penultimate quaver, such as the D sharp of bar 4.

The left-hand quavers outnumber those in the right hand and need an equally smooth *legato*. The small slurs indicate the groups, but keep the overall phrase lengths in mind.

Sudden changes of dynamics can be overdone. Bar 9 could cause some raised eyebrows if too enthusiastic, and the dynamic levels need to be watched throughout, particularly in the last two lines. A quieter moment from the second quaver of bar 21 would be helpful, or the end might become too thunderous.

Chord playing and *legato* touch do not easily go together. It helps to keep the upper fingers firmly connected from bar 10 onwards. The inner parts ideally need to be joined but don't show as much. Synchronization of hands might be a challenge for some pupils, especially at the cadences. The tempo should flow on evenly, not allowing for 'comfort rits' – the slowing down to find the notes – when chords arrive at the phrase ends.

This piece is titled 'Harebell' in Gurlitt's original set.

B:5 T. F. Kirchner *Prelude in A minor*

The term *legato* may need to be explained and demonstrated at regular intervals in these early stages. It is such a household word to musicians, but relatively few candidates show that they really understand it and can make the singing, connected sounds needed here.

Each hand contributes to the smooth melodic lines and the ends of slurs are not lifted, just 'thought', while the four-bar phrases expressively unfold. Matching and listening to the tone is important throughout, and the little *diminuendi* need careful planning.

The bass-clef entry at bar 9 comes as a real surprise but shouldn't be over-emphatic, as warmer tones are called for from bar 13, leading to the climax at bar 17. The tied E from bars 9–12 is held throughout, and the accented dotted minims from bar 13 are still sung, not 'stabbed'. Do make sure they last the whole bar.

Pupils often overlap notes when trying to join from finger to finger. The hidden part-playing is the technical core of this piece and needs to be managed while building graceful expressive lines in each hand. Examiners will hear when the intentions are good – even if some gaps or uneven corners show that work is still in progress – and they are realistic about what can be managed in these early stages.

B:6 Schumann *Stückchen (Little Piece)*

Teachers will recognize this as an old friend. The piece has appeared in examinations for many years and still sounds as fresh as ever. Common problems also recur through the generations and the left-hand quavers can easily get 'upside-down' in relation to the melody. Lots of left-hand practice, using some rotary or rocking action, will help to find a smooth flow, avoiding bumps on the thumb notes. The change of position in bar 7 may cause a lurch while the low F is found.

With twice as many notes in the accompaniment as the melody, balance is an issue. The left hand needs to provide a gentle background, responding to the rising and falling of the phrasing, but never being overpowering. The warmest tones, around bars 11–13, should not upset the lyrical mood. The double bar at 8 is not a break, just a tiny comma. Encourage pupils to listen for exact co-ordination, as the left hand can easily get slightly ahead.

Examiners will be delighted to hear four-bar phrasing in both hands, and musically alive pupils will be able to bring spontaneous touches to the melody – tiny moments of *rubato* within the main beat that immediately show the budding musician, rather than a dutiful learner. These subtleties are born, not made, but demonstrations will help to set alight this instinct, turning a familiar teaching piece into something special.

C:1 Absil *The Stream*

An unusual and captivating piece, portraying an ambling stream wending its way gently down the hillside. The image is enhanced by the irregular phrase lengths, which not only give the piece a timelessness but also provide a useful point for discussion; it is never too early to begin considering form and structure in preparation for the musical discrimination tests in later grades. The main difficulties of the piece are capturing the 'sound world' and keeping the articulation even. Otherwise, there is little to worry most pupils here.

It is a calm piece, no torrents or waterfalls, and both hands should be *legato*. The danger of spoiling the character will come from the left-hand accompaniment, where a heavy E will quickly destroy any feeling of ease. In fact the semiquavers need to be a little lazy, particularly the bottom notes, and held on just a touch longer than marked under the E to give them a sense of line. Too much rotation of the hand should also be avoided; this is the surest way to throw weight on to the thumb and give the left hand a limp. Instead, the thumb *controls* the note, with the weight staying primarily towards the outside of the hand.

The right-hand melody needs just a little more brightness to the sound, achieved by keeping the hand rounded, using the ends of the fingers, but still maintaining a *legato*. Some listening practice will be needed at the end of every tied note to avoid an unwanted accent on the following quaver; the sound must be matched carefully here. The same applies in the final two bars, where the left hand needs to be carefully graded to stay out of the way of the natural *diminuendo* of the right-hand A.

C:2 John Hawkins *Donkey Drive*

Before looking at the notes of this humorous and characterful piece some dancing around the room, use of percussion (bought or homemade) or clapping will be needed. The comic rhythms imitating the wilful donkey should provide much scope for fun-and-games, but if you are anticipating introducing the piece to a pupil, do allow a lesson or two to secure the timing aurally before throwing in the extra difficulty of playing the notes.

Fortunately, the hands move together in the first line and all that is needed is the right attack: a crisp, light *staccato* from the surface of the key with some bounce at the wrist. Hands fall very comfortably over the notes and there are no large jumps.

The donkey and cart almost get going from bar 5, interrupted by the rather irritable 'ee-aw's. Some separate practice will pay dividends here, making sure the right hand is *legato* between the chords and using the rests to contrast the *forte* brays.

The tempo suggestion is excellent – probably no faster than this though. Ensure that the rests are not clipped before the comic *piano* end and that the hands are held over the keys for the final three beats of the last bar. A broad smile whilst playing would not go amiss and will help communicate the comic nature of the piece.

C:3 Pamela Wedgwood *Strawberry Flip*

If your pupil is an Aswad fan, a street dancer, learning to play the drum kit, or, best of all, has a friend who is learning the kit and can play along with them, then they should have little problem with the reggae rhythms in this piece. Others, however, will need a lot of help establishing the groove as the performance needs to have an extremely steady pulse and an instinctive feel for the syncopated quaver chords in the right hand. It might help to use the reggae beat on an electric keyboard as this will also reinforce the significance of keeping the firmer second and fourth beats of each bar. Most importantly, however, play the pupils some reggae music – the performance really mustn't sound too classical.

The middle section is a touch trickier note-wise than the outer sections, but fortunately only one hand plays at a time and there is plenty of time to find the first note of each phrase so there is no excuse for searching for notes. Be wary of the tendency to foreshorten the rests, particularly in bars 8 and 16, where an exam anxiety may lead to some premature entries. The rests are also an excellent opportunity to prepare the hands for the next chord or melodic phrase.

Dynamics and articulation are the key to conveying the musical interest; encourage a good robust *forte* in the middle section and a cheeky *piano* at the end.

C:4 Kabalevsky *Galloping*

Allegro giojoso sounds more like a bracing morning ride than a desperate racing gallop, and the suggested tempo, crotchet = 152, works well. When judging the opening tempo, keep the *accelerando* from bar 18 to the end well in mind and aim to make more of the increase in speed a little later than actually indicated.

Two kinds of touch and a consistent rhythm are the main aims. It's quite hard to keep an absolutely regular beat and immaculate articulation – slurred, then *staccato* in each bar – while keeping the mood lively and showing the dynamic changes.

It's wise to include dynamics right from the start, as the tiny differences of pressure need to be programmed into the finger memory, along with the notes. The first left-hand note of each bar is the most emphatic, with the following second and third beats always lighter in attack. From bar 9 the right hand takes over the main beats, swapping again at bar 17.

Keeping the fingers close to the keys will increase the safety level and as the piece is all in the treble clef, the position at the piano needs to be considered at the beginning of the learning process.

The last four bars are the most exhilarating, but the candidate must stay in control and not fall at the last fence in the heat of the moment!

C:5 Timothy Salter *Cat being bold at first*

Pupils love pieces with stories. The composer writes: 'Cat being bold at first, thinking better of it, going for the prudent option', so decide what to imagine, perhaps writing it in the music over the relevant bars.

The relationship of the right-hand opening semiquavers and left-hand crotchets should be exact. It's all too easy to play the former too slowly and the latter too fast. Counting is essential – just playing by the look of the notes won't produce the continuity or feeling of anticipation. The silent bars are also exact in length. Pupils may miss beats, especially as bar 3 has two crotchets while bar 6 has four. Rests need to be considered as much a part of the rhythm as the notes.

Perhaps the cluster at bar 15 is a sudden moment of fear for the cat, and this left-hand chord needs to last until bar 21 so must have enough substance, helped by the pedal as marked, without being a thunderclap.

Dynamic markings are precise and easy to follow, but if the playing is too quiet at bar 21 it leaves nowhere to go in terms of tone at the end.

C:6 Peter Sculthorpe *Singing Sun*

The composer tells us that a Book of Hours was originally a collection of prayers, for Aboriginal children, to be recited at certain times of the day. Number six is the conclusion of the set as the dancing during the day comes to an end.

Matching tone, passing from hand to hand, gives the melody its evocative mood. Any bumps or hesitations at the changeover would spoil the effect. The quavers flow to the top note of each pattern and are followed by moments of rest, then become more continuous from bar 5, which is not quite as loud as the sunny opening.

The rhythm needs care from bar 9. Make sure the dotted crotchets are the right length, as this figure continues with a *ritardando* achieved by the composer's written time values, made even more telling by the *meno mosso*.

Beware of too strong a start on the first left-hand quavers – they are never on the main beats of the bar. Always give the most singing sounds to the highest notes, which are also marked with a *tenuto*.

Con pedale – but how much? Touches on the first three beats of each bar will warm up the sounds without including the clash caused by beat 4. However, in this strongly atmospheric music, a little blurring is not disastrous as long as the tempo, mood and matching of tone are convincing.

GRADE 3

Pupils should be well into their stride by now and will probably have stronger views on the choice of their programme. The Basis of Assessment shows the same requirements for Pass, Merit and Distinction for Grades 1 to 5, but with the understanding that these elements will be progressively developed through the grades. Different tone colours should be emerging by now, as well as a more confident response to the different styles.

LIST A

Despite the spread of composers, all these pieces have similar demands. A developing sense of charm and elegance is particularly welcome, and balance between hands and awareness of harmonies should also be starting to be part of the playing. A5 is cheeky and lively, needing a particularly good rhythmic sense. Of the set, A6 is possibly the most technically straightforward.

LIST B

B1 and B2 couldn't be more contrasted, although the suggested metronome mark is the same in both. B4 and B5 will suit musical pupils with a sense of line – perhaps those who also play a single-line instrument. Both B5 and B6 are fairly straightforward technically, allowing a more relaxed starting point for the musical ideas to come across.

LIST C

C1, with its repetitive patterns, and C4 are for the technically uninhibited pupils. C5 is for 'cool' pupils, with its jazz feel. The same could be said of C3, although this is slightly more technically demanding. Some pedal is desirable in both. C2 is not as easy as it looks, with good tonal control necessary for polished performances. The advantages and potential snags are immediately obvious in this list; there are no hidden traps.

A:1 C. P. E. Bach *Fantasia in D minor*

All the semiquavers and the *Allegro di molto* instruction could cause this piece to become a race track, with hazards around every bend. It certainly needs a reasonable level of finger facility and co-ordination to succeed, and even more so if the performance is likely to be threatened by nervous tension.

After that gentle warning, be positive about choosing this for pupils who enjoy using their hard-won technique. They are likely to be those who get satisfaction and good marks from even, reliable scale playing.

The first test is the opening bar, which involves covering the B flat with the fourth finger, not a comfortable feeling at the start of the piece, but the suggested fingering really is the best option. After this hurdle, the patterns lie more easily under the hand, providing the fingering is stable and consistent. Some pupils just won't settle fingering, despite various heart-felt marks on the copy by desperate teachers. However, it's unwise to leave the fingering to chance in this style of writing.

To continue with possible problems, the tempo could slacken from bar 6, where hands join together, and co-ordination needs to be under control to hold this passage together without taking too long over the leaps in the right hand from bar 6 onwards.

A stylish account will have a lightly detached bass, plenty of dynamic contrast and a feeling of enjoyment in the playful mood. The *molto rallentando* makes the demisemiquaver run and final trill not nearly as frightening as it looks on the page. It is often the pieces that have taken the most work which finally bring the most satisfaction, and are sometimes played after the exam!

A:2 Blow *Saraband in C*

Do you have pupils who read the treble line quite carefully, but never see the detail in the bass – typical 'top liners'? Teachers will see at once that the bass-clef minims provide a vital harmonic continuity to the slender writing for the right hand. Lots of left-hand practice will help to focus on this, and you can always add the melody yourself during lessons, until the pupil is ready to take over without ignoring the bass detail.

Crotchet =108 indicates quite a brisk saraband, but the piece certainly needs a dance feel, and sprightly dotted notes (double dotted if you like the effect). Do notice that the rhythmic pattern in bar 3 is reversed in bar 6.

Blow may well have had his own problem pupils, but he did have the privilege of teaching Purcell. Musicians of that era would not think twice about including trills – they were all part of the enjoyment – and perhaps the small print these days makes them look more demanding than they really are. In this piece, the semiquaver trills highlight the main points of the four-bar phrasing, as well as adding extra polish. Fortunately, it is easy to use the stronger fingers, starting on the upper note in each instance. The rhythm must tick away regularly; watch for any slowing up, except perhaps at the final cadence.

Examiners will be delighted to hear dynamics and phrasing contributed from the left hand. This can have a surprisingly powerful effect, and it's helpful to imagine 'layers of sound', the left hand shaping the music in parallel with the right hand, but always discreetly at a slightly lower level. Perhaps even Purcell needed occasional reminders about such refinements from his eminent mentor.

A:3 Dandrieu *L'Agréable*

Couperin and Rameau have eclipsed Dandrieu, whose name may be unfamiliar to you. He too was a celebrated French harpsichordist of the early 18th century, and this pretty, pastoral gavotte could be imagined as the elegant background music to a lavish outdoor party of the period.

There is a suggestion in the footnote as to authentic handling of the slurred quavers, but many candidates will play these evenly, as printed.

The left hand needs to trust its keyboard geography, as there are some changes of position and clef which need confidence in performance. The slurs are editorial and add to the style; they only need a gentle releasing of the last notes, giving definition to the groups and helping the hands to be exactly synchronized. The lines of quavers are almost equally important when coinciding in each hand in bars 3, 11, 14 and 15, but the left hand should be gentler when accompanying, such as bars 4, 5, 8, 9, 12 and 13. There are some quite gymnastic corners at these points, which will respond to practice.

The cadential ornaments are not too demanding and there is no need to change the fingers as written; use whatever works safely within the rhythm, or simply play mordents, starting on the beat.

The dance needs a sense of fun, underpinned by a regular pulse; the opening two upbeat crotchets, typical of a gavotte, should be played lightly. The *forte* marked may cause too heavy an attack, especially for those who are familiar with rock and pop. Go for the lightness, clarity and precision typical of harpsichord music (which must have been much less disruptive to the neighbours when outdoor parties were held in the 18th century).

A:4 J. S. Bach *Minuet in G minor*

This is a real gem, as one would expect, although don't be too influenced by the title; this minuet is more an aria than a dance and has a very personal melancholic expressiveness. Try playing the pupil one of the slower dances from the cello suites as an introduction and explore some of the more contrasting minuets in *The Anna Magdalena Bach Book of 1725*.

It is not a fast piece; around crotchet = 66 works well, but it is not without its tricky moments. The left hand needs to provide a warm, harmonic support so pupils will need to be aware of all held notes, whether on top or underneath. This can only be successfully achieved if they listen to the ends of notes and perhaps occasionally glance at their hands to double check.

The notes of the right hand are straightforward, but there are a few surprise intervals so it will need consistency of fingering to aid the memory, and tonal control to avoid unwanted accents. Encourage the pupil to sing the melody whilst playing the left hand to aid fluency and musical shape. They might then write in the larger phrase marks to help identify the musical structure.

It is the care given to the beginnings and ends of phrases which will give the melody a vocal line; accenting the first note of each will interrupt the musical flow, but a 'tapered' beginning will give musical direction. Similarly, a delicate *decrescendo* at the end of a phrase will anticipate a small breath and give the performance some space. The semiquavers should be unhurried and eloquent.

Most important of all, discourage a strident or mechanical 'one-dynamic' articulation. The melody does not need to be entirely *legato*; some subtle phrasing will enhance the performance, but it needs to retain an elegance, charm and poignant beauty.

A:5 Kirnberger *Polonaise in D*

If you have already played this polonaise through you will have realized that it is a cheeky and rather unpredictable piece. It has a perky character but will need some getting used to structurally.

It does contain many of the classic features of a polonaise – the divided first beat and the two-bar phrases finishing on the third beat – but this phrase structure will feel quite unfamiliar to most pupils at first. Some conducting practice would help the pupils enjoy, and feel comfortable with, the irregularity. There are, in fact, three two-bar phrases at the beginning and end, and an extended four-bar phrase in the middle section, creating a rather nice symmetry – part of the charm of the piece. In performance these phrases respond well to being clearly distinguished by a gentle lift and *decrescendo* at the end of each.

The piece is also a little quirky technically. There are unpredictable corners and it will need some lively articulation in both hands. Experiment with articulated, lightly detached semiquavers, perhaps phrasing together the first two of some groups. Note the athletic jump in bar 9 of the right hand.

A lot of separate practice and pupil/teacher duet work will pay dividends; insist on musical character and buoyancy throughout. Consistency of fingering will make note learning quicker, and giving each phrase musical direction will aid the physical memory. It is worth noting that the last four bars are a repeat of previous material so there are only 12 bars to learn.

Once secure, this will be a good piece for confidence as the processional nature of the polonaise means that it will respond well to a firm tone and there are classic moments for echo effects. It shouldn't be too fast and needs to be played with a smile and technical freedom.

A:6 Mozart *Menuetto II in F*

A charming and slightly coquettish minuet, the melody of which wouldn't be out of place in a Mozart opera. It requires a lightness of touch and a subtlety of articulation and dynamic shape to convey the character, but it is relatively straightforward technically.

The danger spots can be seen at a quick glance. The semiquavers should be even, shapely and not slow the pulse, and the repeated notes must not sound mechanical. It will be worth spending some time on both aspects, asking the pupil to practise the runs in a multitude of different characters – perhaps *staccato* (from the surface of the keys), with gentle accents, in small 'sprints', with a variety of dynamics and from memory.

With the repeated notes, the first decision is fingering. If the fifth finger is used throughout, then there is the danger of them being laboured and becoming too heavy; changing fingers, however, does make learning more sophisticated although it helps the control. 5-4-3-2-1 works suspiciously well.

Apart from this, the essence of the piece is not hard to grasp. Light left-hand chords and quaver accompaniment are essential, as is a lightness and *decrescendo* at the end of each phrase. Be wary of the heavy thumb in the right hand after the double bar. There should not be too much rotation in the hand here and the tone of the top notes is controlled with the fingers so that they are given a sense of line.

No virtuosity or drama is necessary here – just an elegance and naivety. This is an excellent choice for a musically sensitive pianist.

B:1 R. Fuchs *Proud Horseman*

The proud horseman of the title has a certain dignity which would be lost at a wild gallop. The tempo indication catches the ideal speed, but it takes more than that to convey the character of this miniature portrait. Try demonstrating the piece at the same tempo but in two different versions: one with innate vitality and the other without. Pupils will pick up on the difference straight away, whereas it is hard to put such subtleties into words.

Aim first for a light but positive touch – nothing too thick or heavy – and take every opportunity to contrast the articulation. The slurs show where a *legato* line defines certain patterns, and the passage from the last quaver of bar 14 through to the pause at bar 17 could be exceptionally smooth.

The left-hand rests are important and co-ordination must be exact in order to keep the rhythm precise. Common difficulties will be late left-hand chords and uneven rhythm, caused by the effort to keep the hands together. The finger changing is not necessary. It's possible to keep the first quavers light, even if the same finger is used for both. This applies several times in the piece.

Little dynamic variety is printed but there is always the opportunity for tonal imagination and the rising and falling of pitch will also contribute. The *rallentando* leading to the pause at bar 17 is a moment of calm before the theme returns, this time accompanied by even left-hand quavers. Avoid any slowing up here and keep the left hand very light.

The piece does need a good facility to succeed and also the ability to combine neatness with a crisp canter.

B:2 Glinka *Mazurka in C*

Teachers will spot the Chopin connection here and they may wonder if this pupil will eventually be playing the famous mazurkas of that composer. Glinka has given the Grade 3 player a delightful introduction to this nostalgic style and pupils will take to it immediately. Isn't it a bonus when you don't have to say, 'Well you *will* like it when you know it better...'?

Control of tone is an issue here – a lovely warm *legato* needs to be found. Robust players with more determination than delicacy might be wiser to choose a less vulnerable piece.

The dance feel is helped by leaning on the first beats in the opening phrase, with the left-hand chords arriving gently on the third beats. The acciaccaturas may look frightening but are the easiest of ornaments to bring off and they really catch the character, so do help pupils to include them early in the preparation.

It is interesting to distinguish between the *legato* quavers and those marked semi-*staccato*, bars 11–12, 19–20. These are detached in a relaxed way, not as short as a real *staccato*. There are quite large stretches in bars 9 and 10 and also when this pattern returns. Those with very small hands may find these awkward and it's important to be prepared about a bar ahead.

All the musical detail is significant and although it's quite possible to play the piece without pedal, examiners will be delighted to hear touches of pedal or *legato* pedal changes at bars 9–10, 13–14, 17–18 and 21–2. The rests will be sacrificed but the colour will benefit.

The *moderato* in the tempo indication should be taken to heart. This is a gentle dance, full of expression, yet always poised.

B:3 T. F. Kirchner *Poco lento*

Composed with obvious affection for his grandchildren, this one deserves to be played with love and care. It's a gem of a melody, with a duet-like effect between the hands. Throughout the piece, the pupil needs to listen to the tonal levels, and balance the accompaniment against the melody, which sings out clearly in its different clefs.

Pupils might misread the rhythm at the start; if the semiquavers are played too quickly the time signature becomes three-in-a-bar instead of two. It's worth settling that safely before solo practice starts as wrong habits are hard to overcome later. The four-bar phrases suggest a gradual increase of tone to the peak of each one, and examiners will be delighted when this happens as smoothly in the left hand as in the right.

The changing positions when the melody appears in different clefs should be inaudible in performance. We're all familiar with the anxious gaps that can break up a melody, so pupils will need to practise their keyboard geography so that they are not left searching for the notes.

The lyrical climax happens in bars 11–12. A little broadening of these quavers will make the expressive point, and musical players will feel how touches of *rubato* add grace to the moment.

The arpeggiated chord in bar 14 should take a little more time, and allow the next melody entry to follow clearly, despite being heard much lower in pitch. Although not marked by the composer, students might include an *a tempo* at the end of bar 14, before slowing up again for the last two bars.

Pedalling as printed really helps the mood and colour – it would be rather dry without, so give this one to young candidates whose legs are long enough and whose musical sensitivity will make their own grandparents appreciate their efforts.

B:4 Karganov *Arabesque in B minor*

Perhaps this is a beautiful duet between a cello and violin, at first melancholy and remorseful, then more optimistic and cheerful, but finally descending into sadness again. Disguised within this lovely piece is, of course, an exercise in *cantabile* playing, pianistic balance and *rubato*. The melodic lines need a reliable *legato* and some weight behind the fingers to produce a positive singing tone, while the accompaniment should be very soft and not too short. A supple wrist and slightly flatter fingers will help achieve a less edgy tone on the chords.

The piece can be effective without pedal, but it is much more so if some is used. This said, great care must be taken in bars 2, 16 and similar bars not to catch the dissonant notes, so 'play safe' and only use it in bars where the notes are fairly consistent with the harmonies (such as in bars 3, 4, 7 and 8).

There is no technical athleticism here so there are few problems except perhaps the jumps in the left hand, which might just need a quick glance at the keyboard for orientation. If this is the case, make sure the pupil knows where the eyes are to return to on the score.

Some eloquent rhythmic flexibility and dynamic shape is essential. Encourage this early on in the learning of the piece, if not immediately, and develop an expressive freedom with the pupil before adding the accompaniment otherwise there is the danger that it will 'beat time' rather than follow. The melody must communicate; follow the *decrescendo* in the first two bars and perhaps shape the second phrase to the middle. Putting words to the tune will help, but only if the pupil is then encouraged to imitate the rise and fall of the voice on the piano.

Encourage lots of breadth, time around the musical corners and technical ease; a successful performance should have the audience 'smiling through their tears'.

B:5 A. E. Müller *Serenade (Allegretto) in G*

There is really no reason to separate a minstrel's song to his beloved, or a ballad by George Michael, from this serenade, and many reasons to relate them. All have a single purpose, to convey to a listener the performer's feelings, whether it is to attract someone's affections or in the hope of a bar of chocolate. The appealing melody therefore needs some words in mind to help communicate it; not sung out aloud, but sung by the piano with the same nuance of dynamic, shape and conviction.

The only difficulty thereafter will be developing the fluency and lightness in the accompaniment to achieve the correct balance, and the most common problem will be a heavy left-hand thumb; there are lots of Ds and they could easily become very intrusive. It is best to think of the bottom notes as a complementary melody (or backing singer). Shape the accompaniment to the melody, keeping it just a little softer, and avoid turning or rotating the left hand on to the thumbs as this will not help the control.

Another typical danger will be a strident tone and a four-square rhythmical approach. Pupils are often so nagged to play in time that they find it very hard to develop an ebb and flow. Break the mould by exaggerating the *rubato* and then encourage a more refined flexibility. The *poco ritardando* and mini-cadenza need lots of time and just a little rhythmic freedom will make such a huge difference to the performance and make the song just that bit more personal and special. Have fun with a pupil, finding out just how much is possible here – 'holding' the listener's attention before the return of the tune.

The piece should not be played at too slow a tempo. Crotchet = 112 will work well.

B:6 Rebikov *Pastoral Scene*

A captivating and delightful little piece, it has one of those tunes that haunts the memory and inspires images of rolling hills and green pastures.

It doesn't present too many technical problems once the left-hand fifths are learnt. Don't miss the opportunity here for some aural work and for relating it to reading skills. For example, if the pupil can pitch and read fifths fluently then they are already halfway to hearing and understanding cadences.

The most awkward moves here are in the left hand in bar 5 and in similar bars; the accompaniment needs to be as fluid and *legato* as possible here without any hint of accenting so that it doesn't intrude on the melody. There are other instances where the left hand jumps (bars 2–3 for instance); these need to be noticed and the moves anticipated so as to avoid any hesitations and to practise controlling the tone. A fast-moving hand will often accent the note if the jump is slightly panicked.

After this, the melody must flow effortlessly and gently over the top, with plenty of dynamic shape and rhythmic elasticity. No 'snatching' or accenting the ends of phrases except for the occasional emphasis on the second beat. Be careful here; these should be more like joyful dance steps or skittish sheep than violent foot stamping and should always be within a dynamic context.

Observe the various tempo indications. The *più mosso* is a change of mood but not a change of gear; grade the *rallentandos* sensitively and make sure the *tempo I* really is *tempo I*.

There is a sleepy end to this piece. It needs a well-controlled *rallentando*, a sensitive blend of harmony on the final chord and a long, still pause which should keep the audience in suspense. Barely a breath should be heard until the pedal and hands are lifted.

C:1 Kabalevsky *Playing Ball*

This is one for candidates who have good finger facility and like playing from memory. It's ironic that pieces with titles suggesting games are often quite hard to play, and planning where to look up and where to play from memory will be important if wrong turnings are not to be taken. The first notes of each bar are the key to memorizing the patterns.

The finger changing indicated at the beginning of the piece is not necessary, as long as the repeated notes are kept light and neatly defined. The rhythm of the piece must survive the various changes of position, and practising in short sections with a real focus on the inner pulse will be an important part of the preparation.

Notice that the pattern is inverted at bar 9 onwards and that there is another change at bar 17. These geographical changes help to divide up the piece for practice purposes.

Do point out that *crescendo* means to start at the current dynamic and then gradually get louder. So many candidates start *crescendo* at *forte* and have nowhere to go, with resulting hard tone.

Once again vitality is essential and the little slurs and *staccato* help to give this lightness of attack. The tempo needs to be carefully judged so that it's lively enough, without crossing the safety line into the danger area. Continuity of tempo and rhythm is the key; do watch the single dotted crotchets at bars 32 and 38 – they could so easily be cut short.

Candidates need to keep a firm rhythm, a cool head and a sense of fun, right through to the last quaver.

C:2 Peter Maxwell Davies *Safe Landing*

Hopefully, not too many youngsters will begin to learn this at home without noticing that the left hand begins in the treble clef. It sounds almost feasible at first in the wrong clef, but very much better where intended! Tiny hands may find the chords in sixths difficult, so check this before starting work.

It's harder than it looks to keep an absolutely even crotchet pulse at this easy-going *andante* tempo. Many teachers will be writing 'steady' in large print over the opening bars. Keeping hands close to the keys and a small neat *staccato* action will be helpful, as the right-hand chords must maintain an exact pulse while the left hand does some quite complicated things. Watch the length of the first left-hand semiquaver and similar figures later. This could easily be too long or too late and the details – slurs, *staccato* and *legato* – all need to be included for a polished performance. Bars 5 and 6 are easier to play from memory than looking at the page, but looking up again at bar 7 is important.

Sudden changes of dynamics add bright colour, and the *crescendo* from bars 10–12 marks the climax. Pupils need to be alerted to the right-hand quavers at bar 12 – many will tend to carry on playing crotchets. Fitting in the left hand here will take some careful practice.

The chords in sixths should lie comfortably under most hands and bounce along lightly in a cheerful mood. The crotchet pulse ticks on through the last two bars, with the rests being part of the rhythm, but place the final chord carefully to round off the trip.

C:3 Mike Schoenmehl *Melancholy*

The first thing that will strike candidates trying this is the clash between the right hand G natural and the left-hand G sharp in bar 1. 'That can't be right . . .' is likely to be the reaction and in order to make the best of the first week's solo practice, teachers would be well advised to explain the mood and sounds so that the pupil starts with the right ideas.

The composer tells us that the accompaniment should be considerably quieter than the melody, and of course in this idiom the 'swung' approach will work well, although a straight version is equally acceptable in examinations. Whichever the approach you choose, the right hand needs a good *cantabile* sound, with plenty of emphasis on the first beats and an ability to keep the melodic thread clear when chords are played, such as in bars 3 and 8.

The bass minims do need to be held and it may be that pupils with larger hands will be able to take the inner crotchets with the right hand, which makes it easier to sustain the bottom line. Most, however, will play it as it's placed on the page, which works equally well, providing the minims are held as long as possible.

The section beginning at bar 9 implies a question, followed by the answer in bar 10; a spontaneous, improvised feeling is right at the heart of this kind of music. A *crescendo* from bar 10 to bar 12 would work well and leads comfortably back to the *mezzo forte*, when the main theme returns.

To come off really well the piece needs to be played with a sense of performance and strong atmosphere, ending with nicely spaced-out chords in the final bar and the quietest possible top C at the end.

C:4 Bartók *Wedding-Dance*

This is definitely not the refined dance of the bride and bridesmaids, but rather more boisterous and uncouth – possibly the groom and his uninhibited friends!

There is little subtlety here but it does need a confident, yet not too harsh, tone, good articulation and some dynamic shaping if it is not to sound too strident and ugly. The sound will come from plenty of arm-weight behind firmly supported fingers, coupled with a forgiving wrist. No rigidity allowed!

It is a deceptively tricky piece rhythmically. Don't be fooled by its appearance; lots of aural work will be needed to train the inner ear before committing the notes to the physical memory. A few incorrectly placed chords in the early stages will take some undoing and relearning.

There is also likely to be quite a lot of 'searching' for notes if the rests are not used wisely. Consistency of fingering (whether as written or your own) is essential, and some practice playing the chords to a crotchet pulse (i.e. ignoring the rests) will help to encourage the hand to get ready instinctively and quickly, regardless of when it is due to play.

Notice the *tenuto* marks above the chords in the first line and *staccato* above the left-hand chords. Bartók knew the modern instrument and one could be pretty certain that this is to ensure that the chords last a full beat. Those in the bass clef will naturally have far more resonance and need more time to clear, particularly for the rest.

The tempo (crotchet = 96) seems absolutely right – it certainly shouldn't be any faster – and remember that *forte* is a range of dynamic, so use this, particularly in the melody, to give the three-bar phrases shape and melodic direction.

C:5 Mike Cornick *Mellow Fellow*

A 'cool' and nonchalant little number – the sort of tune one might whistle, thumbs behind the lapels of your jacket, while strutting to the end of Southend Pier.

The notes are not difficult and it falls very comfortably under the fingers. The success or otherwise of the performance will depend entirely on achieving a convincing interpretation of the detail, a characterful 'swing' feel and a relaxed, casual tempo.

As far as detail is concerned, there are several features to look out for. Firstly, don't insist that the grace notes are too 'classical'. They are with the beat and should not be too slow – some just 'squashed' lightly together with the main note.

Secondly, notice the *sempre legato* marking. The small phrase markings dictate a light and shade to the line; they should not be articulated as you would for Mozart, but simply implied.

Thirdly, observe all the dynamics and condition them into the memory so that, even on an 'off-day', they will still be there. Some pedal will help colour the piece; it is not essential but enhances the atmosphere, so if a pupil is happy to experiment then don't dissuade them.

The swing feel involves a little more than just playing in triplets. Listening to jazz is the only way to fully appreciate the slight rhythmic emphasis often given to the shorter note of the swung rhythm and the elongation of the beat. Some scat singing, (doo-bah) for the less self-conscious, would really help.

Finally, keep the tempo steady and expansive. Many pupils will feel the temptation to rush and the performance may well get faster over time. This could lead to some insecurity in the last line and destroy the 'mellow fellow' image completely. There was a Sixties song called 'Mellow Yellow' – if you can find it, play it to the pupils. It has exactly the right feel, will save a lot of explaining and the title is just a little too close for coincidence!

C:6 Koechlin *Le Ruisseau limpide*

A brief look at this deceptive piece may give the illusion of something relatively easy for the grade. It is a gem: an unusual, appealing and pictorial piece conjuring up a fleeting image of a small, clear stream flowing through green pastures, the occasional splash over a rock.

It is not as easy as it looks though. The control and tonal nuance needed cannot be easily taught; every quaver needs to be dynamically graded and the line should be beautifully shaped without a hint of stridency or deliberate articulation. Using the more 'padded' part of the finger and feeling the way along the key surfaces will give the sense of seamlessness and help the finger stay on the key a little longer. It is marked *très égal* but just a little overall fluidity to the phrase will be needed to convey the movement; do use the *piano* range to give it dynamic shape – not just where marked.

The left hand should be as unobtrusive as possible and the substitutions observed to enable this. Virtually no pedal is required in this piece so there is nothing to help the *legato* here.

Any hint of unevenness, the occasional accent or too much tone will spoil the image, so absolute fluency is needed. Surprisingly, perhaps, lots of practice *staccato*, in rhythmic groups, and the accenting of notes in threes (not always the first of each group), will all help attain absolute control. It is often fun to change the title ('The Raging Torrent'?) to challenge the pupil technically and make the actual character much more marked in their mind.

Remember that the piece finishes more softly than it begins so it should not start too quietly; hold the final note for its full length before gently lifting the hands and leaving the listener with an image to remember.

GRADE 4

Although it is possible to use the pedal from Grade 1 onwards (providing children can reach it), most pupils begin to use the sustaining pedal on a regular basis by the time they reach Grade 4. The two forms, direct and *legato* pedalling, both potentially feature in these lists, particularly in List B, which continues to have the more warmly expressive pieces. Grade 4 is generally thought of as the last of the 'baby grades', after which technical capability and musical awareness are rather more integrated.

LIST A

By this time, we hope that pupils are beginning to think beyond the technical demands. All of these pieces have some 'finger medicine', but should not come across as if that was the only consideration, even if it has been the main focus of practice. A2 needs a sense of drama and fun, while A4 is an expressive, elegant choice in this list. A5 is for good scale players, and A3 is not too much to learn, but needs a variety of different touches – perhaps for a pupil with a slightly melancholy disposition? There are some ornaments in this one, and also in A6, but nothing too frightening.

LIST B

A vivid imagination and sense of ebb and flow can be exploited in several of these pieces, particularly in B1 and B4. B5 has a melody projected across an accompaniment in the same hand, quite a developed skill. B3 might suit a romantic teenager with a good ear for balance, while B6 is quite easy in its technical demands, but depends upon really colourful, imaginative playing.

LIST C

Some of these are technically quite straightforward, but do look beyond the notes for the musical message. C4 has some tempo changes to contend with, and C2 is for quick, intelligent pupils, who have a bright sound and musical conviction. C3 is in the jazz idiom and the notes are not too difficult, and C5 has different rhythmic demands in order to create the strong, rustic feel. Safe counting, in different time signatures, is also the starting point of C6, but the atmosphere is completely different from that of the previous peasant dance.

A:1 Beethoven *Allemande in A*

Do not confuse this playful allemande with the stately, slow dances of the Baroque era. This is, in fact, a very different composition altogether – more a ländler and three-in-a-bar feel. There are two contrasting sections: the first has a smiling and carefree elegance, the second is more bombastic and slightly disgruntled.

The technical difficulties are almost exclusively in the right hand of the first section, where even articulation is essential. Plenty of variety in the practice will be needed here: a light *staccato*, some rhythmic work, accenting alternate notes, deliberate tone etc. The pupil will need a pliancy of the wrist and to avoid wild swings of the elbow which so often create unwanted accents. Consistency of fingering is vital, and memorizing would help take the mind off the mechanical detail.

The technical demands are, of course, entirely subservient to the musical demands. An eloquence and rhythmic freedom, together with an integral dynamic structure, are needed to give the melody shape. The dynamic markings are very appropriate and an excellent starting point.

The second section is more straightforward technically, although the left-hand semiquavers in bar 20 may need a little attention, particularly as it is necessary to hold on to the bottom A to enhance the harmony. From bar 33, 'lean' into the *tenuto* notes with a relaxed wrist, and lighten the upbeats, making sure that each of the repeated bars has musical purpose – in this instance each is progressively louder until the *forte* is reached.

Make sure the pupil is used to the *da capo*. Don't leave it until a few days before the exam to practise it.

A:2 G. Benda *Sonatina in A minor*

A sonatina of contrasts: one part grumpy, reminiscent of a loved but slightly unpredictable grandfather, the other a more cheerful and slightly remonstrating grandmother. The lively grandchildren are running wild around the house and taking life lightly until they are finally told off in bars 43–4. Well, it's one possible way in to a wonderfully eventful piece.

This piece is eventful in technical terms as well, and bars 17–22 should be considered very carefully before it is given to a pupil. Some will manage these semiquavers with only a little effort, for others it may be their Achilles heel and they should avoid the piece if there is any likelihood of insecurity and unevenness here.

The secret in this passage is to make the left-hand semiquavers very short, getting the hand quickly out of the key. This will also help to brighten them and give a sense of line and direction. The right hand needs to be controlled but very light; a slightly flatter hand may help and allow more room for the left hand, which will need to leap nimbly over the top.

Elsewhere, a good, relaxed technique is needed to enhance the phrasing, and clear articulation will help to keep the piece alive. This will be particularly true in the more robust opening, where a slightly detached touch will give this energy; contrast this with a charm and refinement in bars 5–7 and elsewhere.

The texture and register could encourage a rather harsh tone in the wrong hands, so the *forte* should be interpreted as 'positive' rather than 'loud'. Even in the *sforzandi* in bar 43 a certain amount of constraint is needed. In order to achieve the contrasts, lighten the *piano*. Don't forget to practise the *da capo* long before the exam, taking just a little time over the quavers which link back to the beginning.

The piece may be *allegro* but do not take this as an indication to 'drive' the music forwards; it needs some space around the corners to communicate the tongue-in-cheek seriousness.

A:3 Telemann *Presto in E minor*

Pupils attracted by this dance-like *presto* will be delighted to know that of the 40 bars there are only 24 to learn; the opening eight are repeated three times. Despite its tempo marking, this is a slightly melancholy piece, marginally cheered by some major tonality in the episodes, but it definitely conveys the sense of a dancer who can think of something he or she would rather be doing than trying to dance a cheerful gavotte.

A whole variety of touch is needed throughout to convey the buoyancy but, fear not, most of the phrasing is matched between the hands. In bars 2–3, for instance, the detached third and fourth beats and phrased first and second can be choreographed together to great effect, particularly if the suggested detached left hand against the right couplet causes some unease. The triplets in bars 12–13 will need to be fluent and effortless and are, of course, a classic moment for the pulse to slow, so instil a firm sense of pulse in the pupil here.

The main cause of anxiety is likely to be the ornaments. Do remember that if they cause too much angst then leave them out. Most problems occur though because pupils have too much weight behind the fingers or are pushing into the keys in their determination to play them. In fact, by their very nature, ornaments convey an accent so need to be kept much lighter than preceding and subsequent notes. Pupils will benefit from practising with a small pause before the ornament, lightening the hand and then playing using fingers only. The release of weight will quickly become instinctive and free the fingers for what follows.

Experiment with the marked dynamics but, above all, encourage dynamic shape to every phrase. Many performances are likely to have a 'here are the notes accurately played' air about them, but there is little need for this. Enhance the character with a lightly articulated approach and demand much more musical interest and direction even within the context of a few notes.

A:4 Cimarosa *Sonata in G minor*

In the midst of the smiling charm are two passages which could cause the moan: 'If it wasn't for those few bars…'. It's frustrating when 80 percent of the piece is coming along beautifully only to slow down and stumble when awkward semiquaver runs don't come up to the standard of the rest. Go straight to bars 7–11 and 15–20 and decide on suitable fingering. The printed suggestions work, but try also 3-2-4, beginning on the E flat of bar 8 and 3-1-3-2-5 from the high B flat of bar 15, as starting with the fifth finger on black notes can be dangerous. It depends, of course, on the stretch and facility of each individual. The jumps in bars 15 and 18 are helped by the lifted ends of the previous slurs, but any uncomfortable gaps in the flow will need to be overcome.

The tiny fragments connected by slurs are part of longer four-bar phrases. The first gives the pattern with its peak on the first B flat of bar 4. The middle quaver of the three is always the most important and has a gentle emphasis. Rests form part of the graceful conversational character – the last quaver should be cleared on time.

Despite its minor key, there is an extrovert quality about the mood and the printed dynamics are beautifully judged. The left-hand details are important for a stylish account and the main three-quaver idea is passed from hand to hand, bringing a question-and-answer spontaneity to the theme.

A safety measure is to think of the tempo of the semiquaver runs before starting the piece – a purposeful but dignified walk sets this delightful little sonata on its way.

A:5 Haydn *Finale–Presto*

'I acknowledge with pleasure the desire of many music lovers to own a complete edition of my piano compositions…' So begins the foreword, signed by Haydn in 1799. He would surely also be pleased to know that many candidates worldwide are choosing them for their exam programmes.

The clear scale patterns and open look of the piece are attractive, and there are no hidden perils, providing the technical level makes even semiquavers achievable. Excellent articulation does not mean the over-aggressive 'machine gun fire' attack occasionally heard, but rather a smooth, well-matched stream of tone, graded into elegant phrases, each with its main point at the end in typical Classical style. A firm rhythm helps to avoid a headlong rush, and will also ensure that the longer notes at the end of each run are not shortened.

No dynamic indications are printed, so feel free to devise your own plan. The left-hand minims from bar 9 need to be held, giving a firm basis for the change of texture. Co-ordination at bars 11 and 12 may be a problem for some; a little 'rotary' action of the right hand will help and should prevent the thumb note from being too obvious. A lovely even flow of semiquavers passing from hand to hand is the aim from bars 15–18, making sure that the first note after each change is evenly matched – no false accents disturbing the calm at this point.

With too much weight on the first note of each semiquaver run it sounds as though the bar lines have moved, so think towards the main beats of the bar to establish the real pulse, which anchors the performance reassuringly for both player and listener.

A:6 D. Scarlatti *Minuet in A*

Are you a footnote reader? Some are attracted to the small print at the bottom of a page but pupils usually go straight into the music. The suggested phrasing may look off-putting on the page, but works easily and stylishly, with the fingers tending to make these patterns quite naturally. The bass-line quavers could be either *legato* or detached, but in either case the quavers should be lighter than the crotchets. The bass-clef rests are a stylish extra in a polished account.

Give this one to pupils with a taste for detail, precision and elegance. It trips along at quite a lively minuet pace, but still has a real dance feel about it – think of aristocratic footwear, rather than rubber boots, if encouraging someone who has a rather robust attack. The 3/8 time signature gives the one-in-a-bar rhythm, so different from a more pedestrian three beats.

A lack of printed dynamics can either be stimulating or worrying. Examiners accept workable alternatives and when nothing is printed, please don't assume that the piece should all be played at one level. The harmony helps these decisions: the naturals from bar 7 add a gentle touch, while the sharps have a brightening effect.

A potential rhythmic blurring could set in from bar 7 and in similar patterns, if the first three notes are played slightly too slowly, giving an effect of a triplet, rather than the crisp two semiquavers printed. If the last two quavers were hurried, this would also unsettle the beat.

The cadential trill at bar 17 is quite easy to slip in and another in the same form at bar 35 rounds it off with a flourish.

B:1 Bridge *Miniature Pastoral No. 2*

The piece is not without its technical difficulties and if it is to be performed with sufficient flow and flexibility then it will need to feel comfortable at a faster tempo than the ideal to allow that extra confidence.

The most demanding section is bars 17–36, where the difficulty lies not in the notes, but in ensuring that they are held for their full length. Separate practice and work without pedal is required. There are effectively three instruments playing here and each part needs its own identity and musical shape. Memorization will help.

Balance and pedal are also important. Careful listening is a must in the opening to avoid the accompanying chords becoming too intrusive. This is not hard if the approach to the keys is gentle. A 'snatched' action, perhaps encouraged by the *staccato* markings, would be totally inappropriate and give the chords a bright edge to the sound.

Pupils may find the control less easy in bars such as 5–8, but keeping the weight behind the thumbs and avoiding too much rotation of the hand will help the control. In the middle section note that the ear will want to follow the top line, so project this. The moving inner part will be heard anyway but too much emphasis on this will attract the ear and disjoint the line. Pedal where marked but do not exclude it elsewhere; it can be used from the beginning to provide a more atmospheric sound.

Providing it is given musical significance, a pupil will enjoy the chromaticism and subtle grading of dynamic. Work with them to achieve a natural *rubato*, perhaps pushing on to the middle of phrases and relaxing to the end; never allow them to lose sight of the strong images portrayed in the piece.

B:2 Heller *Study in B flat*

It is always best to give a study an imaginative title and this is likely to be played with far more colour and more musically if the pupil can come up with their own. Perhaps 'Contentment' or 'A Summer Breeze' might be a good starting point for discussion.

The 'study' required is that of listening to pianistic colour, rhythmic freedom and tonal control, particularly through repeated notes. There are glimmers of a tune in bars 17–22 and it is worth pointing these out, but it is the shifting harmonies that convey the movement and warmth. Don't be deceived by the hat accents; they are not a sudden strike with a reprimanding ruler – more a glockenspiel joining in just to highlight specific notes.

Begin by asking your pupils to play the harmonies alone and explore the changes in mood – these are particularly obvious between the first bar and bar 9 for instance. Then add the repeated notes. These will need to blend in with the harmonies, providing a fluidity and movement but definitely not 'beating time'. Changing the fingers will help move the hand naturally to the next chord.

Bars 23–34 should not be dismissed as an irrelevance; they need a vocal shape and musical integrity far more meaningful than the simple B flat major scale might suggest.

Any rigidity of pulse will be to the great detriment of the piece; lots of *rubato* is needed to enhance the mood and character. For example, time needs to be taken over bar 23 and over the spread chords in the second bar of the coda. Elsewhere, pupils should follow their instincts, adding pedal throughout, and giving the impression of improvisation.

B:3 Grieg *Arietta*

A very beautiful and poignant aria, almost definitely a love song, but if your pupil is not into this yet, then perhaps ask them to muster up the same passion that they might employ when appealing to their parents for the latest computer game or sweets. It can often have just the same persuasiveness in drawing out musical subtlety.

Strong third, fourth and fifth fingers in the right hand are required here to project the melody. You may need to spend some valuable lesson time working at balancing two notes simultaneously in one hand, as it is the independence within the right hand that will be the key to a successful and convincing performance.

Right-hand only practice, complete with semiquavers, will reap rewards but bear in mind that the semiquavers will need to be velvety soft to allow the melody to sing through. It is not just knowing that one finger plays faster into the keys than the other, it is remembering the 'feel', and mentally preparing the approach to the note; so point this out and if they haven't experienced the sensation before don't expect it to happen securely over night. Once the balance is understood and appreciated then it is down to good, *legato* pedalling (changing with each new harmony), musical shape and ebb and flow. Lingering a little in the middle of the opening phrases (not every time though) and taking time in bar 9 are possible moments of *rubato*.

Otherwise, keep the song gently moving and do, as always, put some words to it to encourage some spontaneity and awareness of phrases.

B:4 Dunhill *Study in F*

Easy on the ear but harder on the fingers, the chromatic notes make the patterns of this piece more difficult to grasp than straight split-chords, so some memory work on the left-hand opening notes of each group will save time and keep the music flowing smoothly. Having F, B natural, B flat, A, then D, F, E, E in mind, gives the foundation of the patterns which should of course be evenly divided between the hands, avoiding a bump on the higher-pitched third semiquaver. Think on to the next group as if there were no bar lines.

The melody comes out of hiding at bar 9 and the left hand needs firm fingers to phrase and project the line, with its changes of articulation. The accented As appear the same on the page but the fifth one, at bar 11, is the most important – the others lead to this moment, which introduces a change of texture. Touches of pedal help here but clear it for the *staccato* quavers, keeping the right hand *legato* in contrast.

Balance of hands, evenness and the phrasing which is indicated by the *crescendo* and *decrescendo* marks, are all musical aspects that examiners will hope to hear, and the tiny *ritardando* and *a tempo* at bar 21 will be a significant moment.

The delight of this piece, when played fluently, will repay the effort of getting to grips with the opening bars. The *allegretto* indication, more relaxed than *allegro*, but not as slow as *andante*, is just right.

Make sure the piece finally glides to a halt, with sensitively placed last chords, and restrain the urge to rush on to the next piece.

B:5 Granados *Dedicatoria*

There is nothing of the rough and tumble behaviour of typical young boys in this tender little dedication to Granados' son Eduardo. Perhaps it's an expression of his own paternal affection, rather than a portrait of the boy himself.

As with all *cantabile* melodies with an accompaniment in the same hand, the technical aim is to keep the harmonic background at a gentler level than the *legato* top line. No easy task when the outer weaker fingers carry the melody and the heavier thumb has to be carefully controlled. A sensible starting point would be to practise the melody and bass alone until quite secure, then practise a phrase at a time, putting in the quavers. The *legato* pedal at the start should be continued throughout.

The middle section (bars 9–16) contains a couple of awkward moments where the right-hand intervals could cause a hesitation and the dotted quaver–semiquaver patterns in bars 10 and 12 need to be neatly managed within the rhythm. The semiquavers could easily be a little late.

A tranquil yet flowing tempo is suggested (unusually, at the end of the piece). This will catch the mood, and musical pupils will be able to bring touches of *rubato* and a sense of direction to the lines.

Candidates with ease of expression and good awareness of the 'weighting' of notes will enjoy this one. It's a lovely melody, needing familiarity with *legato* pedalling for a really polished performance.

Granados expresses a lot in just one page. As so often with these miniatures, the challenge is not so much learning the notes, as what the player brings to them in terms of sound quality and musical response.

B:6 Maikapar *Clouds*

It might be wise to have a suitable photograph to hand when you introduce this one to your pupils. A skyscape, preferably rather dark and gloomy, will catch the imagination and immediately set the scene for some mood music.

The time signature 6/4 is sometimes misunderstood in terms of pulse. Here it's best felt in two and the tempo suggestion also helps to avoid a plodding effect, which would make the wrong sort of heavy weather of the music. Co-ordination and *legato* need to be priorities – no gaps in the line and no left hand anticipating the right – a frequent pianist's trap.

Don't miss the short 'octave-lower' sign in bar 4, and at this point a tiny relaxing of the tempo into the new idea at bar 5 would be a bonus if not overdone. The held dotted minims from bar 7 need a firm, warm tone to last their full length. The left-hand chords from bar 12 also need a certain substance to support the change of colour, which brings a more translucent effect to this central section. The hands are very wide apart at bar 16 – always potentially disconcerting – but do point out that the right-hand notes are the same but an octave lower in bar 17, which make the ledger lines at bar 16 much less frightening.

The printed dynamic range lies between *piano* and *molto pianissimo*, but the actual pitch of the notes adds sonority and the piece is never flimsy in tone. Examiners will hope to hear the chords from bar 26 lasting their full length and if the final low B flat fails to speak, simply play it again without giving the game away – it will sound even more atmospheric!

C:1 Hindemith *March*

This is a playful and toy-town piece full of self-importance and mock-seriousness. It is not hard to play; hands phrase together, there are no wild jumps, few problems of control and in fact it should be a joy to learn and to teach.

The first problem encountered may be unfamiliarity with the sound world – and this may dissuade some pupils from finding it immediately appealing. Some scene setting before playing it through will help and the teacher's own enthusiasm will play a big part. Otherwise, the hardest bar is probably the first, keeping the left-hand notes *legato* underneath a non-*legato* melody. Some slow practice, consolidating the independence of the hands and listening to the contrast, may be needed.

Clarity of articulation and a rock-steady pulse will convey the march-like character. The quavers work best *staccato*, unless otherwise marked, and the couplets need clearly articulating; dropping the wrist on the first and lifting on the second will give an ease and consistency to the phrasing.

Pupils will need to appreciate the phrase lengths and shape them accordingly in order to avoid relentlessness creeping in. Try, for instance, a slight *decrescendo* towards the third beat of bar 2, a slight breath before the next half of the phrase and a *crescendo* through to just before the *fortissimo*.

Point out the bugle call in bar 13 and the slight pompousness ('chests out') at the end.

C:2 Nielsen *Jumping Jack*

This is a clever and effective composition, evoking the effect of a small, concertina-shaped firework (probably now banned) which, when lit, lies on the ground sparking and then suddenly explodes, leaping in unpredictable directions and at unexpected intervals. The piece will suit a quick reader and intelligent student; it also needs confident and clear articulation to convey the flashes and sparks.

It would probably be wise to approach the final eight bars first. These will need to be learnt from memory, both aurally and physically, to enable sufficient fluency. The *staccato* touch will come from close to the keys, active fingertips and a quick attack, the hands almost imitating the jumping firework. For once, take the *fz* literally; a bright sound here will help colour the picture, as will vivid dynamics. Once the final eight bars are learnt then the rest should prove no problem; many bars are repeated or similar in pattern.

Rhythmically it is not as complicated as it looks and quite repetitive, but it needs a lot of exaggerated 'pulling around', almost grotesquely so, to capture the erratic nature of the firework.

A great piece for showing off to friends, for family concerts or music festivals and, as an experiment, pupils might like to play it unannounced and then ask for a suggestion for the title to see how effective the performance was.

C:3 Christopher Norton *Fifth Dimension*

This is a somewhat cheeky gem, the title reflecting the interval upon which the piece is based. It has some surprising harmonic shifts and an almost nonchalant air. There are no technical dramas here though and it should present few problems to most pupils – just a couple of slightly awkward jumps.

The piece is very distinctly straight-eights and perhaps slow-rock in style; it will respond to an improvisatory feel and a cheerfulness in the opening. The grace notes need charm and should be lightly 'squashed' together with the chord, although not too meticulously or Classically executed; the *staccato* needs to be fairly short. This is in contrast to the small rising motif, which needs to be musically shaped and very *legato*.

The dynamics are crucial and the piece is likely to lose all its appeal if it is too *forte*. It needs casualness about it and the tone should be carefully graded to suit this. It is the balance between the hands that will ensure the immediacy, keeping the top notes of the chords brighter and a *cantabile* tone in *legato* phrases. Lighten the second and fourth beats considerably to avoid a four-in-a-bar feel and 'place' the longer chords.

A minimum amount of pedal is marked but extra pedal can be added to warm the longer chords – just a 'dab' for the first three beats of the second bar, through the minims in bars 15 and 21 and the semibreve chord in bar 16. This will make a big difference, as will some pedal in the final bar.

Otherwise, keep a fairly stable pulse except at the end, think two-in-a-bar and enjoy the harmonies. The piece should almost play itself once sufficient freedom and fluency are acquired.

C:4 Eleanor Alberga *Only a wish away*

Some composers leave you in no doubt as to what to do with their music and you will find at least one instruction in most bars of this piece – wonderfully reassuring, especially in a contemporary style. 'Doing as you are told' will not produce the mood and sense of performance that the title and delicacy of the writing deserve, but at least it makes a good foundation from which a more fanciful improvisatory feeling can grow.

Go for rhythmic accuracy first, including the composer's tempo changes and adjusting the pulse accordingly where the new metronome marks are printed. Silent beats are also exact.

At least two kinds of touch will be necessary: a smooth *legato* with a little *cantabile* on the longer notes for bars 1–8 and similar passages, and a neat, detached clarity for the *staccato* moments. The pedal is marked where needed; don't be tempted to add more.

Problems in this piece are likely to be rhythmic, and some counting in quavers may be needed for bars 11–13 and 24–8 until they become reliable. Tonal control is also a high priority. The texture will not take any harshness in the *fortes*, and the lighter moments need firm fingers to avoid a misfire when notes fail to sound, especially on an unfamiliar piano. Some dynamic contrasts are sudden, such as bars 5 and 15; others give a chance to grade the tone.

The different sections are clear from the appearance of the music although the piece should still sound as if it is a natural progression of thoughts with a purpose and destination. Pupils usually have open minds about contemporary sounds, linking them to their imagination more readily than mature learners.

C:5 Veselin Stoyanov *Bulgarian Peasant Dance*

Bulgarians obviously like to dance in irregular time signatures. Teachers who know the many dances of Bartók will recognize the style and vigour of this piece, which can make a terrific impact.

The time signature 5/8 is relatively unfamiliar in Western Europe, but the feel of the rhythm should appeal once it has settled into the mind and fingers. There is an extra kick, sometimes marked with an accent on the third quaver, which adds bite to the beat and helps to avoid the common error of holding the last quaver too long, turning the time into the more familiar 6/8. Watch the bars with a dotted crotchet for this trap, and make sure the bar lines are crossed over without hesitation. The tempo indication is ideal, and the rhythmic emphasis is the strongest characteristic of the piece.

Bars 1–4 introduce the mood and suggest a drone-like accompanying instrument which continues through much of the left hand. Pupils may like to imagine the dancers gathering in their colourful national costumes. These thoughts can help to keep the playing alive, especially as the repetition needed for effective practice can drive out the mood of the piece, leaving safe notes but nothing else.

The passages where the left hand has *legato* quavers need to be watched for any slowing of the tempo (bars 37–40 and again in the last section from bar 56). Watch the quaver rests, such as from bar 9, which add emphasis to the offbeat chords.

The *crescendo* at bar 37 is only to *mezzo forte* at bar 41 and it is worth noting that, despite the robust character, the dynamics are not all that loud – bright and crisp but without heaviness.

C:6 Carl Vine *Semplice*

'Simple in effect, but not easy to achieve', will be many teachers' reaction when considering this choice. Pupils of all ages will certainly need to count in quavers when practising the changing time signatures. A fraction too short on the crotchets, or too long for the last quavers of many bars, and you've lost the metre. Early planning of strategies will avoid the wrong habits, which frustratingly tend to be more quickly grasped than the right ones. Watch, especially, the places, such as bar 2, where two crotchets are followed by a quaver rest – it's so easy to hurry these moments.

Pedalling as marked will add warmth to the tone and give a little more sonority to the first quavers, which colour the harmonies. Although the smaller two-bar sections have a shape of their own, the direction flows on to eight-bar phrases and these need a sense of overall structure.

No dynamics, except at the start and end, are printed, but the tone will naturally vary a little with the phrasing. The quietest bar is potentially bar 16, with a thoughtful pause, and the reappearance of the theme at bar 17 could be a little more positive than at the opening.

Each bar will need individual practice from bar 9. Searching for a key will not help, as the sevenths never resolve, but the notes themselves are not hard to play.

Avoid falling into the trap of being too quiet too soon near the ending. The longer notes create an even *ritardando* but need careful control to avoid disappearing entirely before the final chord. Once mastered, this one could well be 'exam-proof', with an uncomplicated mood and technical demands well within the grade.

GRADE 5

Grade 5 is a watershed between the early grades and those beyond the necessary hurdle of Grade 5 Theory or Practical Musicianship. Hopefully, the extra demands, both technical and musical, have been gradually approached through the preceding years and it will be apparent to teachers which of their pupils is capable of progressing successfully on to the later grades and which might be reaching their natural limits. In either case, enjoyable performances of the pieces for this grade indicate a real ability to play, rather than just early attempts at the instrument.

LIST A

Good independence of hands is a requirement in many of these pieces, and repetitive bass patterns occur both in A2 and A6. A1 and A4 are quite exposed, but the actual notes are not too demanding. A3 has the advantage of an extremely famous melody, which always gives confidence in performance.

LIST B

There are lots of different styles here, and musical imagination is needed in all of them. A really crisp rhythm is vital in B1, while B4 requires some spaciousness and time in the performance. An ability to play neat right-hand thirds is the starting point for B3, and in B6 an experienced use of the pedal is a help.

LIST C

C1 is ideal for dreamy pupils with a sense of colour, but C4 is for the diligent ones, with clarity of tone and articulation. C2 is quite unusual, and needs good left-hand control; give C3 and C5 to the musically responsive who display sensitive use of the pedal. C6 is technically straightforward, with a strong jazz idiom, and needs virtually no pedal.

A:1 J. S. Bach *Prelude in D minor*

A one-in-a-bar feel and independence of hands are the starting point. Lots of separate practice is usually required in Bach, and although the piece looks approachable, it is wise to allow plenty of time to assemble it.

Slurs and dynamics are editorial suggestions. Slurs in bars 1–4 might also apply to other bars which begin with the same three-note figure. Unmarked quavers can be lightly detached, which also helps to keep an elegant lightness. The suggested tempo is reassuringly manageable, but it could be taken faster in confident hands.

The two printed ornaments could be learnt as an integral part of the right-hand line, rather than put in later, avoiding possible disruption of the pulse. The demisemiquavers continue through bar 4, fitting in at double the speed of the left hand. The decoration in bar 23 also works as printed, starting on the F, but is slightly more likely to cause an uncomfortable moment. Deal with it early on, or leave it out if the problem refuses to yield to treatment.

Fingering will need a lot of care, and the printed suggestions are one approach (and, yes, you can use the fifth finger on the E flat of bar 9; it is much the simplest solution).

A dynamic plan in harmonic sections should be in place as soon as the notes are under the fingers. After a positive start, bar 9 could introduce a quieter section, with the dynamics rising again with the pitch around bars 17–19, then returning to *mezzo piano* by the double bar. Printed dynamics on the second page work well, and the ending could either be strong, or gentle.

The rhythm and lilt of the piece will survive any small blips providing that accidents are not made worse by an emotional reaction. As ever, the teacher's attitude can make or break the performance, even though they are not present in the exam itself.

A:2 Diabelli *Rondo*

Give this delightful little movement to pupils who have good keyboard geography and finger facility. It is not for the dutiful plodders, despite the encouraging look of the printed page. The changes of position, hand crossing and lively tempo all contribute to the technical demands of the piece, but also to its obvious charm.

Allegretto for a third movement in 6/8 should have a sprightly mood, resisting all temptation to slacken the tempo when the patterns change. All the articulation marks are important for a stylish account but should be played as if they had just occurred as a happy idea, rather than painstakingly achieved over several months.

The detached quavers (in either hand) are not aggressively *staccato*, so fingers will need to be close to the keys with a small controlled action.

Legato left-hand quavers will be helped by some rotary action, and the simultaneous contrasting *legato/staccato* touches need independence of hands and awareness in practice.

Hand crossing is a big issue in this piece. The secrets are to know where you are going and to arrive in plenty of time in order to ensure safety. It's best to memorize the passages from bars 16–24 and 40–48, but also to practise where to look up again. Nerves can play horrible tricks at these moments, unless the physical habits are firmly in place.

Two small details to consider are the right-hand crotchets in bars 9–10, which are not at the start of the bar, and could turn into unintentional accents, and also the figuration in bars 24–6, which could momentarily unsettle co-ordination.

The last two lines need rhythmic control to avoid a dangerous *accelerando*, and accidents on the chords. This section should dance along in tempo, punctuated by left-hand rests (so easy to overlook these), and the *crescendo* is best started quite late, reaching a triumphant *fortissimo* at the end.

A:3 Handel *Air in F*

What a pleasure it is to meet such an old favourite in the exam syllabus. Many pupils will have heard this famous air from the *Water Music*, but it is always helpful to play them an orchestral recording when introducing Handel's own keyboard version. You may come across contrasting performance styles in the record catalogues: quite brisk and very dotted, or, with more dignified and relaxed, almost triplet, patterns. Either approach is musically effective; just choose your preference and keep it consistent throughout. Do read the footnote about the rhythm.

Almost hidden under the famous melody are passages of part playing where held notes need finger contact and *legato* to maintain their lines. Examiners will be able to hear whether this is managed or not; again, separate practice from the start will put this in place.

The poised four-bar phrases reach their peaks at the ends, often with a graceful ornament adding to the point. These could be played as written, or simplified into mordents started on the beat. Recorded versions will be reassuring in this aspect, as you will hear various ornamented performances and some played without any decoration at all. The phrasing is the thing, and the left hand can make a positive contribution here, rather than just playing at the uniform *mezzo forte* that we often hear in exams. The editorial dynamics scheme is varied enough to give structure without being over fussy but it's not the only alternative. This is never a loud piece – warm and firm at times, gentle and restrained at others, but always with a sense of courtly grandeur.

Keeping a really regular pulse with all the subdivisions neatly within the individual beats will probably be the main task, while the simplicity and perfection of the melody shines through the dots and through the centuries.

A:4 J. C. F. Bach *Allegro in E flat*

This happy-go-lucky and cheerful *allegro* is essentially a duet between the hands and needs a fluent independence and charm in order to convey its character.

Begin with the editorial fingering and phrasing, using this as the basis for exploring other possibilities. The fingering in particular will make or break the performance, not only because it will need to facilitate a smooth effortless sense of line but also because any hint of ambiguity or lack of consistency will result in weak points in the fabric of the performance.

It will be valuable to do lots of teacher/pupil duet work in the early stages, with the shape and direction of phrases clearly defined to give the piece a sense of structure. Think in terms of a very slow one-in-a-bar, keeping the second crotchet beat light; around crotchet = 76 will work well.

The opening phrases seem to want to go towards the first quaver of the second bar, so avoid accenting the initial semiquaver. Controlling the key from the key surface will help the control; pupils may be inclined to 'throw' the hand at the first note and create an accent here.

Grade the dynamics carefully for the next few bars, perhaps with a *diminuendo* as sequences fall and a *crescendo* as they rise. Keep the cadences (and turn) light and buoyant. The tone should never become too *forte* as the textures cannot support this.

Technically, once notes and fingering are learnt, slow practice will be needed in small sections, if only to co-ordinate the phrasing between the hands. Some pupils may find it difficult to detach one hand whilst the other is *legato* but it is always easier if it is educated into the fingers from the very beginning. The semiquavers should be very even and cheerful.

With careful preparation and an instinct for the character, the piece is musically very rewarding.

A:5 Dieupart *Gigue*

A strong sense of pulse, confidence at the keyboard and good articulation are just three of the main attributes needed to convey the character of this joyful yet slightly arrogant gigue.

Don't be put off by the apparent complexity of the ornaments; they are not intimidating, and although the printed suggestions should be considered, a simple grace note or mordent will suffice if necessary.

If the piece is learnt with care then it is not particularly difficult. The performance will rely on the harmonies created by the longer notes held under or over the moving parts (such as the top line in bars 16–17), so these need highlighting before a pupil begins to learn the notes, and appropriate fingering insisted upon.

The stream of quaver movement could be daunting to a pupil but the gigue falls beautifully into phrases and the editorial commas show clearly and effectively how to think of the melody. Notice that the phrases are sometimes two- and four- and sometimes three-bars long. Giving appropriate dynamic shape and articulation will enhance them. Resist the temptation to phrase every group of three quavers by slurring together the first two and therefore making the second and third quavers short. If used throughout this will lead to too many 'first' beats and a rather heavy dance. Instead, experiment and explore with the pupil how, by selectively using the couplet phrasing and at other times keeping the three quavers entirely detached, much greater length to the phrases can be implied.

A good, bright tone will enhance the opening. Perhaps take the opportunity to drop down in dynamic for the minor tonality, building up through the sequences. Do experiment with block dynamics but don't be too fussy; it is better to concentrate on overall shape and keeping the upbeats and ends of phrases light to allow the gigue its charm and energy.

A:6 Mozart *Rondo*

If you can find a recording, then an exploration of the *Divertimenti for two clarinets and bassoon* would be an excellent introduction to this jaunty and cheeky rondo. The articulation of the woodwind instruments is reflected in the writing, and if a pupil had this in mind, it would greatly enhance the character and save a lot of explaining.

Don't be put off by the relative length of this piece in comparison with others in this group; it is, after all, a rondo, with the bonus that quite a lot is repeated. It will be important to consider the technical demands though. Most pupils will have encountered the Alberti bass by now and be reasonably in control here, though it does need a lightness and agility as it is quite fast. It is probably the *staccato* chords from the A minor section onwards (bar 40 onwards) that are likely to be laboured in an otherwise sprightly performance. A good, relaxed wrist is needed here, responding to an active fingertip. It is essentially wrist *staccato*. Any rigidity will at best sound wooden, at worst tense up the forearm. The music needs to 'laugh' its way down.

Phrasing in general should be carefully observed and obeyed, but try not to encourage these outside a musical context. Attach musical significance to every articulation mark: an aside here, a laugh there, a joke or flirtatious comment elsewhere so that they are understood as well as played.

Dynamics are also in plentiful supply. The tone should not be too harsh or heavy in the *forte* so bring the *piano* down significantly to help the range. Use a playful variety of tone in repeated phrases (such as from bar 17 onwards) and allow a little rhythmical flexibility to enhance those typically cheeky *appoggiaturas* and surprise harmonies.

A convincing final performance will have absorbed all the detail in an unobtrusive and musically convincing way and be played with a technical freedom and assurance.

B:1 Grovlez *Pepita*

This dance should be at a controlled, almost hypnotic, tempo – one-in-a-bar, but no faster than dotted crotchet = 52 for real authenticity. The demisemiquaver figures add impact to the peaks of phrases, but need clarity and precision within the beat. Notice that they quite often occur inside a gentle dynamic, which takes more finger control than at louder levels. The right-hand fifth finger will need to arrive promptly on the G of bar 14, and by lifting the final note at the end of the previous bar, extra emphasis is given to the accent.

The *rubato* at bar 17 should not be too indulgent, but almost within the beat, and the theme in a minor key starting at bar 20 calls for a different mood, as there is no change in the dynamic. The 'long' *staccato* marks in bars 24–5 indicate that the note is only just lifted before the next quaver – another characteristic touch. Watch for any slowing of the tempo, though; the piece dances on, despite the sudden drop in spirit. These details are just the same in the left hand from bar 37; some pupils will find this harder to define.

The first page is fairly restrained, but with a strong feeling of the excitement to come. This arrives with a real burst of brilliance from bar 48, climaxing at bar 64, then falling away suddenly at bar 69. Chords in thirds introduce a different mood to the phrases, and here the *rubato* is more insinuating than earlier, picking up the tempo briefly at bars 71–2, where the articulation will need careful practice, then repeating the idea with even more emphasis from bars 73–6. The right-hand *legato* and dynamics are important from bar 77, and the last line speeds up dramatically. The safest plan is to play this from memory, with really firm fingers, avoiding misfires.

Pupils who know the opera *Carmen*, with its vivid characters and flair, will love this one. The seguidilla is in a similar vein – perhaps a recording will add to the inspiration!

B:2 Lyadov *Prelude in D minor*

Teachers who look at the detail before selecting the right piece for their pupils will notice that some finger gymnastics are apparently required. The editorial suggestions include several changes of finger on one note, which is a strong hint that a super-*legatissimo* is the intention. Fortunately, the tempo is slow and reflective, making these potentially awkward movements more feasible. Whether it is achieved by this technique, very familiar to organists, or by dabs of pedal to ease the connection, a *legato cantabile* touch is called for in each hand.

The quavers should form an evenly matched, seamless line, structured into four-bar phrases and weaving between the treble and bass clefs. Avoid giving too much weight on the opening quaver of each phrase, which would have the effect of moving the bar lines.

The piece stays dynamically within a fairly small range, but each passage will have little fluctuations – the *crescendo* and *diminuendo* marks show the way, and the *crescendo* beginning at bar 15 reaches the climax at bar 17 before falling away to the end. The fingering demands in bars 15 and 16 might be just too complex and you may decide to play for safety, changing to 2-3-4-5 in the right hand while taking the lower two notes with the left hand. This piece could be a minefield for misreadings and it is worth checking very carefully before pupils get used to hearing a mistake, subsequently finding it hard to make corrections.

In the right hands this delicate, introverted prelude could be a gem, but the physical control needs to be quite subtle and skilful. The best plan is to give it a try, and even if it is not the final choice, a useful technique will have been introduced for the future.

B:3 Schumann *Italian Fishermen's Song*

The tempo and party atmosphere of the *staccato* quavers seem to portray the fishermen off-duty, rather than casting their nets. Once past the introductory two bars, which may sound like the call 'All aboard!' to English-speaking pupils, the piece skips along merrily, providing co-ordination can stand the pace.

It is surprisingly tricky to play every note *staccato*. There is an almost irresistible desire to slur the second left-hand quavers of each group, but Schumann has asked for the same touch throughout. Synchronization of hands will take concentration and a very close hand position. The nearer the keys, the safer the notes and it will be easier to keep the right-hand thirds under control.

Even at Grade 5, pupils keen to start an exciting new piece could begin the right hand in the wrong clef, but the resulting strange sounds should cause alarm bells to ring before the next lesson. The rhythm of the slow introduction could also be read rather vaguely, but perhaps a certain freedom for the echo is intended, to set the scene.

Stamina will be tested as there is no let up during the two pages. A light but crisp action is the ideal and even if a few right-hand chords go astray, aim to hear the upper line clearly with a natural rise and fall according to the dynamics.

It is wise to keep the examination piano in mind. A heavier action than the familiar instrument at home could be alarming, so some prior knowledge would be valuable before selecting this one.

The last line is a gift for candidates with a sense of performance, and the cheerful mood certainly makes the learning process more encouraging. Schumann wrote at the time of these compositions: 'I don't remember ever having been in such good musical form...', and his enthusiasm certainly comes across in the writing.

B:4 Glière *Morning*

Though by a Russian composer, there is a distinct feeling of Grieg about this piece, and not just because of the title. It is a very evocative and colourful composition, needing lots of space and an ability to 'stop and admire the view'. Pupils should be reminded to give the required number of beats to the first bar and longer notes in bars 3, 22 etc.

The secret to giving the performance a sense of spaciousness is in the listening. The semibreve chord in the opening actually takes on many differing personalities throughout the four beats. With the pedal down the initial immediacy of the notes dies and the tone blossoms like a flower as the other strings vibrate in sympathy and the colour changes. Listening in this way, rather than simply counting the beats, will affect and inform the pupil's approach to the next bar. The balance of melody and chords will need to be finely judged throughout. For example, the quality of the decaying chord in bars 22–3 should influence the tone of the 'dew drop' figures.

Far more pedal is needed than is marked and it would be best to change with each harmony. Do not take the *staccato* dots on the chords literally or imply any disjointedness; the pedal is used here and the chords are gently detached whilst pedalled.

The 'bird calls' in bars 18–21 are not hard rhythmically, providing the pulse is thought of in 12/8, but in any case, do not allow the rhythm to be too rigid here or in the trills. Lots of variety of tonal colour and imagination is needed to conjure up one of those so rare (for most of us) mornings when you can watch the sunrise, listen to the birds and spend time with your own personal thoughts.

B:5 H. Hofmann *Am Abend*

This is a very attractive piece and the notes are not difficult to play. It is, effectively, a musically rewarding study in shaping and projecting a melodic line in three different registers. The important thing to remember is just how quiet the accompanying quavers will need to be to allow the melody to come through, even at the ends of phrases. The balance will seem wildly exaggerated to a pupil sitting at the piano and they will need a lot of reassurance from the teacher as an 'objective' listener.

Begin by just playing the melody of a phrase (with the correct fingering) and exploring the tone, dynamic shape and *rubato*. Then add the quavers slowly and gently, ensuring that the pupil listens to the decay of the melodic notes and never allows the quavers to intrude. Whether they are listening and adjusting will be very apparent in bar 2 and similar bars.

The weight of the hand needs to be supported by the finger playing the melody, allowing the other fingers to control the accompaniment free of any heaviness. Ultimately, the control of the balance is felt in the fingertips and their reaction to the surface of the key, so draw the pupil's attention to this frequently.

The pedalling is straightforward, changing with the harmonies, but the pupil must ensure that they 'catch' the bass notes, leaving no rootless harmonies.

Always encourage sensitive use of *rubato*. If the piece is too rigidly in time it will sound very matter-of-fact and the 'evening' will not have an ease and comfort, more a feeling of relentlessness. This will be particularly significant in bar 33, where the solo melody needs a 'vocal' quality – it's a sort of 'I suppose I had better turn out the lights' phrase, so play it with a big sigh at the beginning, avoiding an accent on the top E.

It may be worth contrasting this piece with Glière's *Morning* and asking the pupils to compare the mood and character.

B:6 Tchaikovsky *Valse*

There is a deceptive beginning to this colourful waltz. It evokes images of whirling dancers, laughter and high spirits. The hosts had obviously forgotten to invite one important guest, however, and the gypsy fiddler enters, ridiculing the dancers by spoiling the graceful three-in-a-bar with grotesque cross-rhythms and the angularity of the gypsy scale (complete with augmented second).

The middle section, though the dramatic centre of the piece, is, in fact, satisfyingly easy to play providing the couplets are choreographed, the hand jumping from one to the next, falling on the first with a relaxed wrist and rising on the second note. This will give you the accent and phrasing.

The outer sections are a little trickier. Practise them without pedal, overuse of which would spoil the buoyancy and phrasing. All the rests and articulation should be clearly heard, but the danger is that the left hand will lack support, so encourage the pupil to hold the bass notes for their full length, phrasing them with the first chord. In bars 19 onwards they must be held with the finger throughout the bar, and given more weight and tone, while the chords are kept light.

Once the piece is learnt fairly fluently then begin to experiment with pedal. The performance will really benefit from discreet use, and in bar 6 the pedal will help phrase the bass note to the chord and colour the second and third beats in bar 19 onwards. Only small touches are needed though, so use with caution.

A broad range of dynamic is necessary, but avoid a percussive or forced tone, coming back to *piano* at every opportunity to underline the elegant style. Take some time also, at appropriate moments, to communicate a sense of cheek and fun, as this, together with technical freedom and panache, will enhance this gem of a piece.

C:1 Brian Chapple *The Blue Pool*

There is no room for doubt about interpretation when the composer gives the instructions. Brian Chapple tells us that '*The Blue Pool* should ripple mysteriously; make strong contrasts between the accompaniment and the right-hand *cantabile* tune, that begins at the end of bar 7'. Advice which combines technical and imaginative directions is particularly helpful, as the two go often together, with the right sound picture creating the appropriate technical approach.

Under the water a regular rhythm still ticks away, giving shape and direction, but pupils in a hurry, or those who have lost track of the underlying pulse, might clip the rests without realizing.

Legato pedalling is essential and is helpfully marked, with special effects at bars 13–22 where sustaining the sounds for two bars adds to the watery illusion. The right-hand crotchets, with their *sempre molto espressivo* and *sempre intenso*, clearly ask for beautiful tone and some gentle *rubato* as they make their delicate connection between the rising arpeggios.

The 'pedal point' left-hand semibreves are always the same and the bottom line never moves from its treble-clef position, giving the piece a lightness of texture and colour. The *crescendo* from bar 12 to the climax at bar 14 is small-scale. The louder moments throughout the piece are very *cantabile* in effect. Watch the tone at the right-hand melodic entry in bar 7; it will take some care and use of the right 'weight' to create a smooth line. The markings over these melodic longer notes show the melody and suggest the effect. They are not accents in the usual sense.

Right from the early stages of learning the piece, encourage a *diminuendo* to the highest quaver, so that the first note of the bar is always the firmest, and the last quaver the lightest. The notes are not hard but tone needs to be controlled at all times to make the most of this choice, which is a gift for sensitive players.

C:2 Lutoslawski *The Grove*

Taken from Lutoslawski's 1945 collection of folk melodies and based on a Polish dance, this needs to be in strict rhythm. Getting faster in the excitement of the moment could be a trap, so thinking in quavers while the notes are learnt would be one way of settling the rhythm ready for the faster performance tempo to come. The touch is clear and bright at *forte* level, while the quieter levels still need firm fingers to guarantee reliability. Pieces with such an economical texture often suffer from too assertive, harsh *forte* passages, or flimsy, nervous, quiet passages with missing notes (and sometimes both problems in the same performance)!

The piece was written just after World War II, when the need to enjoy life and to dance was probably strong, and the music should come over today as a party piece in the best sense.

Finger changing always divides the purists from those making practicality and safety a priority. If the change in the right hand of bar 15 causes the least smudge, use the second finger on both the Ds. The left-hand melody quavers lie comfortably under the hand and it's the rhythmic placing of the left-hand chords that might be a greater sticking point. These need to be absolutely on time and all the same length – just a detached quaver, avoiding an over-anxious semiquaver or a lazy crotchet.

Hectic merriment in a strict rhythm is the aim. The cheeky last two bars need witty placing – no accidents at this crucial moment – and the final left-hand C is the only bass-clef note in the entire piece.

C:3 Mompou *Pajaro Triste*

It's interesting to find a piece which consists of mood rather than melody. The plaintive snatch of a theme never really develops and the repeated quaver–quaver–minim figure simply comes to rest before a new idea appears at bar 7.

If *rubato* has not been explained before, this is certainly the moment to open up the subject and to show how a subtle moving forward then relaxing towards the phrase ends breathes life into the music. The main idea always needs expressive shaping and the *accelerando* passages also have balance as the *ritardando* compensates for the earlier increased movement. It all sounds spontaneous when successfully done but some careful planning of exactly where to move forwards and where to slacken (not too soon in either case) will be helpful. Encourage pupils to think across the bar lines and feel the slow three of the pulse through all the touches of *rubato* and changing dynamics.

Legato pedalling is necessary to make this piece work, and the right-hand *cantabile* should always sing plaintively over the rich harmonies. In the section from bar 7 it is wise to pedal with each change of bass chords; do feel free to use different fingering in the left hand if you find the suggestions at all awkward.

The *sforzandi* marked at bars 7, 13 and similar places are to catch the attention and emphasize the colour. A Beethovenian accent would be overdoing it in this context. At bar 17 the left-hand chord will need to be split – either as an arpeggio or else with the F sharp and C sharp played as a chord, followed by the A as swiftly as possible. Either way, this should be as unfussily managed as possible as it is the upper right-hand melody which predominates.

The falling pitch in all the phrases emphasises the sadness of the title, and the sonority of the bass gives weight to the world-weary feeling, which will be relished by those with a taste for restrained enthusiasm.

C:4 Alun Hoddinott *Lizard*

The poem attached to this composition says it all; it is a descriptive and showy composition and not that technically hard once the pupil has mastered the art of articulating the repeated notes. Don't be distracted by the 6/16 time signature, although it is a clear indicator that some firm rhythmic groundwork is needed before introducing the actual notes.

It is important that pupils don't begin to play the piece without first learning the rhythm. So many bad rhythmic habits evolve from learning the notes before the rhythm. Clap the phrases or play them in a scale until the rhythm is absolutely secure and there is an instinctive awareness of phrases and phrase shape. Then place the notes within this rhythmic framework. The pupil will need to be able to think easily from two dotted quavers in a bar to three quavers in a bar, and then to what is effectively 2/4 at the same dotted-quaver pulse (bar 32 etc.) in order to feel comfortable with the performance.

Fingering needs to be considered carefully and distribution clearly defined; then work slowly through with attention to musical detail but possibly without pedal. Clear articulation of the repeated notes will involve a very quick *staccato*, with the finger coming swiftly out of the key. A light tone will help this as anything too heavy will make repetition impossible for the less experienced, particularly on a sluggish instrument. Use a very direct approach to the key with the finger tip, and remember that it is far better and more effective to hear all of the repeated notes at a slightly slower tempo than half of them at too ambitious a speed.

Persuade the pupil to perform with the broadest range of dynamic in order to encapsulate the image – from the warmth of the sun to the crisp scampering – and allow a little rhythmic flexibility where appropriate.

C:5 Prokofiev *Matin*

This is a wonderful, imaginative miniature in which the Matins bell chimes gently and a mother sings to her child to wake. Most pupils will probably have their own thoughts about the image behind the music, but if played with a real care for the piano sound, balance and nuance it will be a captivating and very effective piece.

Technically, there is quite a lot to consider, but most problematic will be the crossing of the hands in bars 5 and onwards and the large jumps. The piece is not fast – a tempo of around crotchet = 66 will work well if it is sensitively played – but there is a danger of accenting the beginning of phrases if the approach to the key is too panicked. A quick but relaxed jump is needed in order to arrive well ahead of actually playing the notes, so that the beginning of the phrase can be tonally judged and controlled.

The passage from bar 9 as the sleeper awakes could so easily sound unmusical. The right-hand quavers are dream-like, so need overall shape, but should not be too articulated. The left hand needs to project, but possess eloquence, and this will mean being very aware of the sound of the longer notes to help the shape.

Pedalling is not marked but is obviously essential and the ears are the best judge as to when and where to use it. As a guide: in the first few bars try holding the pedal for the first two beats then changing for each of the third and fourth beats. The pupil may also like to consider using the *una corda* in bar 16.

The piece will reward conscientious, careful listening work, but will still require that extra musical sensitivity in order to capture its full enchantment, so this is not a piece to learn just before an exam.

C:6 Pamela Wedgwood *Litter-bin Blues*

A relatively straightforward and problem-free piece to complement some of the other choices. It is not only environmentally friendly but also pianist friendly.

The notes are generally uncomplicated but the problems encountered here are more idiomatic than technical. It requires a real instinct for swung rhythm to fully capture the Blues character. This will first of all mean interpreting the notation, with all quavers and dotted rhythms considered as triplets. It is more than this, however. Imagine a drum kit behind the performer and a doo-*ba* doo-*ba* feel, a slight emphasis being placed on the shorter note. This will go against the grain for many a classically trained musician, but remember that this is not Mozart and the technique for playing this offbeat push may need some encouragement. If in doubt, listen to a Blues pianist.

It may come as a pleasant surprise to the pupil that hardly any pedal is needed at all. The piece works very well without (except at the end), but a lot of attention should be given to dynamic variety, shape and articulation to help give the piece interest. Think 'smoochy' in the *mezzo piano* opening, but aim for a Big Band sound in bars 29 and onwards. It will help here to play long but detached left-hand crotchets and compare this with bar 11 and onwards where a similar touch will be effective.

Clearly, the rests are imperative and the piece should have overall rhythmic elasticity and an improvisatory feel. Although it is not necessary to play it from memory in the exam, this piece presents an excellent opportunity to have a go and an ability to do so would undoubtedly help the fluency and freedom.

Don't be too profound: relax, tap the foot, get into the groove and enjoy the performance with a carefree abandon and ease.

GRADE 6

Reaching this grade means that the pupil has shown strong motivation and commitment, often at a time when school work has also been more demanding. Reference to the Basis of Assessment printed in *These Music Exams* will show how the musical and stylistic elements need to be part of the performance in order to pass at this level. Most candidates who progress to the later grades do, in fact, show their musicality in its various degrees and stages of development. There is now such a wide variety of choice in the syllabus that the emerging musicianship and individuality of pupils can be encouraged and displayed with suitable material.

LIST A
Pupils at this level will be committed to some conscientious practice and care over fingering, which will be needed in all the List A pieces, particularly A1 and A4. A5 is for those more at home in the Classical period rather than the Baroque, and A2 is ideal for quick, alert readers with a sense of humour.

LIST B
It is encouraging to see Brahms and Bruch, with such rewarding musical characteristics, in this list. Both B4 and B5 will be popular choices, and reveal from the first few bars much about the musical make up of the performer. B1 needs a wide range of pianistic colour, as does B6, with its dramatic changes of mood within each section.

LIST C
There is scope for those attracted to the unconventional here. C4 is an obvious choice, with its absence of bar lines, and C6, probably the most demanding of the list, is wonderful for the really rhythmically assured. C5 is relatively straightforward, providing a careful balance is maintained, and age might be a factor with C2 and C3; C2 needs a smoochy seductiveness, perhaps ideal for an older pupil, while C3 will suit younger pupils with ability to take time and explore musical interest and detail.

A:1 Chilcot *Jigg*

This is a tongue-in-cheek dance with some unpredictable twists and turns, no more so than in bar 8 where the cadence in B flat, so very deliberately heralded in the first two beats, is thrown to one side by a rather impish B natural.

Like all dances in compound time, this piece needs light upbeats and subtle phrasing to maintain its buoyancy. It also needs well-behaved fingers. The suggested fingering works well on the whole once the articulation is included, so avoid substituting anything more complex in order to try to keep it *legato* until you have decided with your pupil the phrasing you are going to use. You might, however, try beginning the second beat of bar 36 with the second finger in the right hand and only change the hand position at the beginning of the next bar (third finger in the right hand, thumb in the left hand).

The phrasing needs to be varied to avoid the dance becoming too flat-footed. Clearly it works well to phrase the first two quavers of a three-quaver group, but if used every time this phrasing will result in too many accents each bar. Try phrasing the first and third group in each bar like this and keeping the second and fourth groups detached. In bar 7 and similar bars the pupil could experiment phrasing just the first two quavers and then keeping the whole of the rest of the bar detached; in contrast to the previous bars, this will give more length to the phrase.

The light articulated touch required is achieved by a quick, relaxed 'drawing of the finger tip' along the surface of the key, almost as if getting rid of a piece of fluff which has settled there. This, coupled with a light bounce at the wrist, will give the right control. The couplet phrasing involves relaxing into the first of each group and immediately lightening the hand again. Gently detach the left-hand dotted crotchets where appropriate and avoid too much sound on the octaves as the piece only has a thin texture otherwise.

Some dynamic variety is essential and here is a golden opportunity for 'highlighting' the structure and discussing with your pupil the gradation of tone, perhaps following the rise and fall of the phrases and sequences.

Do feel you can suggest spreading the final chords; it is perfectly acceptable here.

A:2 Mozart *Allegretto*

There is a subtle humour in this piece and here is Mozart at his most mis-chievous. The innocent, cheeky opening is contrasted with a more pompous middle section, followed by chromatic, wicked laughter before the return of the first section. There are so many quick changes of material (albeit related) that the piece will need the sharp-wittedness of an alert reader in order to achieve a good level of fluency. Try beginning with the middle section (bars 23–56) before attempting the outer sections.

Clear, sprightly phrasing will be needed to keep the music sparkling; the *staccato* mustn't be too laboured otherwise this 'lemon sorbet' of a piece will end up sounding like treacle pudding.

From the beginning the overall character will be as much dictated by the left hand as the right, so practise the lower notes of the left hand together with the right, endeavouring to complement the phrasing before adding the repeated Fs. This will be particularly significant underneath the 'written-out' appoggiaturas (bar 1 E natural; bar 2 F etc.), where lingering just a little will add to the charm, providing it is not done every time. The oom-pa octaves in bar 23 and elsewhere are much more straightforward.

The tempo will be important in conveying the character of the piece, and the suggestion of minim = 60 works very well.

Technically, the weak points will inevitably be uneven semiquavers, par-ticularly following rests (bars 13–14), uneasy co-ordination through the right-hand syncopation (bar 3 etc.) and, even at this level, we will hear some labouring of the trill in bar 84. It is far better to use fewer notes and play it fluently than to go for a 'natural' trill and have the pulse falter.

Overall, encourage the pupil to listen actively to the balance. On a strange piano it is not always possible to anticipate the sound, but being able to adjust quickly is an essential skill. It is of particular importance, of course, when the left hand descends into the lower registers, as a modern instrument has far more tone here than a contemporary one, so good adaptability and control is required.

This wonderful music will reward a student's careful and patient work.

A:3 Telemann *Fugue in E minor*

This is a precocious little fugue, more a fughetta. It has all the manner of an adored son showing off his strength in front of doting parents; there are glimmers of the stature of large fugues but it is not quite grown up yet.

It has a motif, rather than a fully-fledged subject, but strangely, if played with slightly tongue-in-cheek seriousness, it works very well. Imagine it played on an organ with a fairly big registration and you'll get the point.

Experiment with the sound of the subject in the opening, slightly detaching the quavers perhaps, and make a feature of each of the subsequent entries, showing off the inversions in bar 2 and making light of the episodes in between. The fifth is the key interval and even in bars 30 onwards the fugue is making a pretence of the subjects entering in augmentation, so play up to the illusion and allow the drama to build to bar 40 where a small *ritenuto* wouldn't go amiss.

Play the passages between the entries at a lower dynamic level and keep the semiquavers light, using the 'hidden melody' to give the piece musical direction and identity (bars 27–9 for example).

Good co-ordination of hands will be needed, particularly in the opening, and well-structured and familiar fingering is fundamental. Ensure that the pupil spends time sorting this out before learning and memorizing the patterns. Lots of duet practice will help achieve a musical and technical freedom, as will some work playing the left hand louder than the right, as this trains the ear and helps develop good independence of the hands.

And so to the ornaments. Some valuable suggestions have been given but do remember that an easier ornament played well is infinitely preferable to a blurred or technically uneasy one, however many notes are included, so feel free to try alternatives. It is suggested that most begin on the upper note, and are primarily in threes, but pupils shouldn't hesitate to play them in twos, particularly in bars 15 and 17, where the problems are compounded by having to hold a note underneath. Bar 17 is a real 'fly in the ointment' as it is not possible to execute a stylish, measured trill beginning on the upper note – so begin on the note.

A good piece for the studious pupil. It will rely on musical conviction and an intelligent interpretation to do justice to the note learning.

A:4 J. S. Bach *Allemande*

It takes most pupils longer than they expect to learn anything by J. S. Bach. The intricacies of fingering, with a lot going on in each hand, can usually only be mastered by practising hands separately – that sensible but often resisted means to a successful end.

Fingering can't be glossed over in either hand and early care pays dividends. Encourage pupils to have a pencil by the keyboard at home and to write their own fingering in the copy. Not only does this show that some thought has gone into the work, but it's less easy to ignore your own instructions than your teacher's, which can become over-familiar. Changes can be made by mutual discussion. Beginning the piece on the right-hand fourth finger may be worrying for some, and 3-1 may feel more secure; thumbs on black keys are fine providing they don't cause a bump, and there are quite a few places where this approach keeps the hand over the keys in one position.

Dynamics tend to arise from the harmonic structure in Bach: the dominant key produces a more assertive effect than a relative minor, so a medium level at the start might drop to *piano* by the end of bar 4, growing with the higher pitch around bar 7 and arriving at the cadence in bar 8 at *mezzo forte*. The new phrase might then begin at a quieter level. On the second page the left hand is even more active. On the last quaver of bar 14 it begins a new idea, to which it adds increasing detail before passing it to the right hand in bar 20. With such interest in the parts, over-fussy dynamics would be inadvisable, but beginning new patterns gently, then building to the ends of phrases, will give structure without distraction.

Ornaments certainly enhance the cadence points, but if you find both decorations in bar 8 too much to handle, omit the first and include the second.

The tempo has a wider acceptable range than some List A choices. Most candidates will perform this one somewhere between a flowing *andante* and a rather more confident *allegretto*.

A:5 J. L. Dussek *Moderato*

You are likely to get a very positive reaction when introducing this sonatina to pupils. The elegant Classical style will appeal to most and the technical medicine is disguised by the charming melody and rippling semiquavers.

The performance tempo (around crotchet = 112) is quite a flowing *moderato*, rhythmically felt in two, avoiding a pedestrian account. The passage work should sound as if easily achieved, although it may take extended practice to become fluent.

Alberti basses have at least two possible difficulties, despite the pleasant harmonic background they create. Awareness of balance is needed as the number of notes in the left hand can easily obscure the melody, and faster figures can cause the tempo to lose momentum. Bar 5 shows the start of one of those places. Some rotary action will ease the way and help to keep the accompaniment light. Whatever the dynamic of the melody, the left hand should be slightly less.

It is possible to make an audible difference between melodic semiquavers, as in bars 16–23, and those that provide a harmonic background (the left hand of bars 5–7): a useful approach, especially for music of this period.

The first upbeat E could become a quaver without the pupil noticing, and you will also need to watch the time values of the last notes of bars 9, 12 and similar places later. The acciaccaturas are part of the melody and easy to slip in lightly. They are not problem ornaments, just delightful extras in the line.

Bars 16–23 and 55–62 are the most technically demanding. There should be no slowing up, and it may take a while to settle the hands together at bars 20 and 21. The left-hand rests help to punctuate the rhythm and should be exact, which is easy to overlook when tackling a tricky passage in the other hand.

The texture of the section beginning at bar 24 comes as another pleasant surprise and the details of articulation are important.

Some pupils will instinctively phrase gracefully and add tiny touches of *rubato* within the beat. It's quite a long piece to sustain and works best for candidates who have good facility plus a musical mind.

A:6 D. Scarlatti *Sonata in D*

The repetitions make this choice much shorter than it looks, which even conscientious pupils will find reassuring. In this style and at this grade, some ornamentation really does belong in the performance. It would sound bare without it and the various editorial suggestions are not too demanding, although you may prefer a simpler form (such as missing out the second triplet of (*b*)). The decorations all begin on the beat and play a part in defining the phrasing, as well as being ornamental.

The alternating five- and four-bar phrases are often repeated with 'terraced' dynamics – all in one block of tone rather than more gradual *crescendi* and *diminuendi*. This imitates the change of manuals on an early instrument and immediately conveys the character of the writing. The tonal contrasts are equally important in the left hand and this line could have detached crotchets, similar in effect to short bows played in a cello continuo.

Articulation should be considered in some detail for a polished account, although an all-*legato* version could also work musically, providing the phrasing is beautifully projected. Try the opening quavers slurred, leaning a little on the first and lifting the second D before an even lighter minim, avoiding a false accent on this beat. The bars of right-hand quavers could all be phrased in twos, or those such as bar 13 could be *legato*; either way works, as long as the pupil feels convinced about the approach and makes it an enjoyable detail.

The repeats should not be played in the exam, especially in a piece as long as this. Small commas, such as at bar 5, are just a 'lift' to show the new level of sound, not a hiatus in the rhythm, which needs consistent buoyancy throughout.

There is a potential danger in slowing the tempo for the syncopations first appearing at bar 19. Keep the bass crotchets absolutely rhythmic, which will ground the right-hand offbeats and prevent muddles.

As always with Scarlatti, a crisp, light but positive touch gives the right sound quality and pupils with a developing tonal awareness will appreciate that a warm *cantabile* should be left for the more Romantic items on their programme.

B:1 J. F. Burgmüller *Cloche des Matines*

This is definitely not one of those mornings when you wake up, groan and hide back under the duvet. It is more like one of those so cunningly depicted in soap advertisements when you are energetically up with the lark and straight under a stimulating shower using the most invigorating of shower gels! The 'bell' here is of course the E flat, which wakes the sleeper, and that wonderful 'shower gel' moment is in bar 17.

The piece is naturally a cleverly disguised study, yet no less attractive for that. The technical difficulties in the opening are two-fold: first, the ability to be able to achieve a *cantabile* top line in the outside of the hand, well projected over light chords; second, the challenge of a large left-hand jump across the right hand and the control of the bell tone.

Most pupils will have encountered the former problem before, although the chords are going to have to be particularly gentle here; the melody is often a single, held (and decaying) note and, with pedal down, the chords will have a natural tendency to build. Plenty of tone is needed in the melody, and the subsequent quavers should actually *diminuendo*. This is best practised without pedal and somewhat exaggerated.

Once the right-hand technique and listening skills are mastered then the left-hand jumps can be practised. Work at these, just keeping the right hand in one position, not necessarily playing anything, then add the right-hand notes as written.

The pedal markings result in a rather abrupt end to each bell strike. Try changing the pedal in the first beat of each bar, allowing the bell to ring right through, but this will require the pupil to hold on to the bass note for its full quaver length to allow the pedal to change.

The middle section (bar 9 onwards) requires good control of the left-hand chords and an eloquently shaped vocal duet in the right hand. Bars 20–24 need particular musical attention if they are not to sound too wooden. Allow the bars, indeed the whole piece, a natural *rubato*.

Bar 25 onwards will be comfortably familiar, but the dynamics should be graded carefully so that a distant *pianissimo* can be achieved at the end.

B:2 Granados *Vals poético No. 6*

This is another miniature gem from Granados, conjuring up wistful memories of that romantic final dance with the partner of your dreams. Definitely a good piece for a love-sick teenager as it needs plenty of spontaneous sentimentality and ebb and flow.

The piece falls into three sections; consider carefully the final section (bar 33 to the end) first. The left-hand arpeggio figures are uneasy if played with anything other than a single hand movement but this implies a fairly large hand in order for it to feel comfortable.

The first two sections, both finishing with a magical, single, heart-stopping note, require a fluid three-in-a-bar but present few technical problems except some independence of the left hand, which will need to know its moves from memory. The melody should be clearly to the fore, but lighten the weight behind the hand for the mordents. By their nature they can imply an accent, so reducing the dynamic frees the fingers for their execution and will not affect the line.

Pedal is needed but is fairly straightforward; generally use it each bar except where the harmonies necessitate a change (bar 4 beat 2 for instance).

Take Granados' markings literally, but do not be afraid to include more flexibility of pulse than marked. It would be particularly appropriate, for instance, to make a feature of those wonderful major/minor changes at the end of the first two sections. Approach the piece with a certain amount of self-indulgence and enthuse the pupils, allowing them to wallow a little in the richness of the harmonies.

B:3 Mendelssohn *Song without Words*

This song may not have any words but it has a poignancy and delightful expressiveness that will attract a more musically mature pianist. Although it may be a little less tricky than some of the *Songs without Words*, it is certainly not easy and requires highly developed tonal control to give the melody shape and to keep the accompaniment unobtrusive. Because of the control needed for each note, consistent fingering is essential, with each finger given its role and 'educated' to achieve a particular pianistic colour. There are some excellent suggestions here but if you have a pupil who is quite comfortable with substitution then do use it, as it can really help keep the hand balanced and prepare it for the next notes.

Weight and speed into the key will be needed to project the melody, but the weight must then be released (although not the note) to enable a lighter, more velvety touch for the accompanying semiquavers. This is particularly important here because they approach the same register as the melody. As a guide, therefore, *diminuendo* as the semiquavers rise, and try to follow the natural decay of the melody. This is best practised in 'slow-motion', the balance and tonal colour just as wanted in performance, but slowly. Every phrase needs a tapered beginning and end and you could spend some time with the pupil conducting the piece through to get a firm idea of the musical structure and direction.

The pedalling is relatively straightforward; change with each change of harmony. Holding on to the bass notes with the fifth finger will enable an unhurried change and help ensure that the harmonic support is maintained throughout.

At no point should the tune be forced or the piece sound too agitated; the suggested tempo marking works well, but as with all Romantic music, sensitively used *rubato* will enhance the beauty and expressiveness so the pupil shouldn't hesitate to experiment.

Even at this stage of musical development putting words to the melody can really help open a window into the music, but only if a real attempt is made to match, in the melody, the nuance and dynamic rise and fall of the voice.

B:4 Brahms *Waltz in E*

At first glance, this looks like a collection of chords and rests. However, a good performance will leave you with a wistful melody, which will stay in your mind for hours. The outside fingers of the right hand have the responsibility of projecting the top line clearly and expressively above the harmonies. This is a skill which needs careful listening, and a slight 'squeeze' with the fingertip, keeping the rest of the hand more relaxed.

It's a useful sight-reading test to play the single melodic line and the bass alone. This will show the pupil what to emphasize straightaway, and help them to define the phrases, which, at one level, are four bars long, but at another extend over the whole 12-bar section.

Based on a waltz (you can also detect the ländler roots in the opening phrase), the rhythm should be fairly disciplined, but of course *rubato* is always present in a subtle form in really convincing performances.

The *piano* dynamics have a certain warmth and sonority. The louder passages expand with orchestral colour, but still within the appropriate limits to the mood – think of *cantabile* strings rather than blazing brass. It is sensible to introduce an additional *piano* at the third beat of bar 25 in order to allow for the *crescendo* two bars later.

The rests are important and add to the cross-rhythm effect as the slurred pairs of crotchets pass from hand to hand. Touches of pedal on the first beat of the bar, releasing with the second, allow this feature to make its point. When the rests disappear, the *legato* is helped by one pedal per bar, but more fastidious players may prefer three changes. The minims still need their full length, and the second-beat resolution should be gentler than the sounds either side of them.

A wide range of candidates will enjoy this: the pragmatic for its shortness and comparative simplicity of notes, while the musically aware will also love its wistful mood and romantic harmonies. They will also sense the ideal tempo (around crotchet = 120), which is fast enough to suggest a dance, but sufficiently relaxed to show the tender little touches on the way.

B:5 Bruch *Klavierstück in D minor*

Max Bruch wrote this piece in his youth, and it's clearly romantic music with a winning melody, but what about the *staccato* bass accompaniment – does this mean no pedal should be used? Not necessarily. A workable compromise would be to use direct pedalling on each set of two left-hand quavers, which belong in the same harmony. Try going into *legato* pedalling from bar 25 to the climax at 31, then returning to the shorter, direct touches for the return of the theme. An all-pedalled account could also be musically convincing, providing the articulation is still kept in mind and carefully judged.

This is not pedantic music, and all this consideration about pedalling must not stand in the way of an expressive, spontaneous response to the lovely melody, which is by far the highest priority.

Pupils who know the famous violin concerto by Bruch will perhaps be able to imagine the violin playing the melody, and the heart of this music lies in that sound quality. The ability to develop and warm the tone on one note is one that pianists envy. We have to 'fake' the effect with a strong imagination, careful grading of tone and mastery of a *cantabile* touch.

After the opening A, match the next semiquaver A to the sound, avoiding a bump after the tie. This is a feature of the piece which will require constant listening to, even when the notes are well-known. Thinking forward to the peak of each four-bar phrase is essential, and here again we find many typical feminine endings with the stress on the penultimate note.

All the first 16-bar section is dynamically gentle, with the *più forte* at bar 9 just coming up to around *mezzo piano*. After the double bar, the relative major key briefly brings out the sun, but G minor, with its tragic romantic connections, is the key for the climax, which will have the right *appassionato* colour, providing the earlier *stringendo* at bar 28 has been really positive. Plenty of sonority in the bass adds to the moment. The single linking bar, at bar 32, falls back to an even more emotional, inward-looking final appearance of the theme. Don't ignore the last *a tempo* at bar 39; we know that Bruch wanted it, and it prevents a potentially sentimental end, which would be just too much of a good thing.

B:6 Grieg *Poetic Tone-Picture*

There is something of the atmosphere of a haunted ballroom in this one. But there are two kinds of dance happening: a French *valse* in bars 1–14, which turns into something more fiery and Chopinesque for the last four bars of the opening section. The dynamic range goes to extremes, so a vivid, colourful performance will need a strong imagination and romantic intensity behind it to really grip the listener. Examiners will know from the first couple of bars if the candidate is really 'inside' the piece, and would always prefer an exciting musical account, even with some small blemishes, to an entirely accurate but monotone performance with no energy in the playing.

Allegro but *non troppo* with a one-in-a-bar feel sets the scene beautifully. The next thing to consider is the style of touch. The bass alternates between a very connected *legato* and detached dynamic quavers for the *con fuoco* section. Above this foundation we have accompanying inner parts, always gentler than the bass, then the lyrical melody at the top, which also has various details of articulation. Touches of pedal work where the bass is sustained, but fingers alone are best as soon as the bass goes into quavers.

There are bound to be some rhythmic wobbles at bars 7–9 until the triplets are exactly the right speed. You may need to point out that the left-hand semiquavers at bar 9 are even, not another triplet.

The middle section starts with a similar motif, then gathers speed from bar 29 into an *agitato* at bar 35, arriving at florid right-hand semiquavers, which in bars 39–42 allow the balance in *rubato* to relax back into *tempo primo* at bar 43. Some pupils will stay cautiously at the same tempo, despite their teacher's urging, while others will rush away, risking stumbles. You have to be bold with the shaping at first, then calm it down later into a more even effect.

Try to find something new in the return of the theme – perhaps a more wistful tone at the opening, then crisper rhythmic bite for a really exciting ending.

C:1 Henk Badings *Rondo–Finale*

This is a cheeky, playful rondo full of sparkle and *joie de vivre*. It is an excellent choice for a broad-minded pupil with small hands and is very well written for the younger pianist. In fact there are few technical problems to trouble the performer, providing he or she possesses good, even articulation and an alert eye. Although the notes themselves are not difficult, it is very easy to miss an accidental or two at speed, so do some aural work with the pupil as they need to know just how the piece should sound, in their head, in order to spot mistakes in their practice. Aim to play 'from memory with the music' to help the fluency.

The piece is very Kabalevsky-like in its sound world and could be a good stepping stone to that composer's sonatinas. The essence of a convincing performance will be in the phrasing; each bar must have its own musical personality. A clean, bright *staccato* and lightness of touch, with a nimbleness of the hands, will keep the opening bars alive and interesting, and this should be dramatically contrasted with the more *legato* and lyrical sections.

Throughout the piece every phrase, however short, should have melodic shape; dynamic nuance will play a big part in adding subtlety to the character. Upbeats must be kept light and repeated notes should always have a sense of musical direction. The actual dynamic markings are limited, but within the *forte* and *mezzo forte* there needs to be a large variety of tone. Bars 23–24 for instance could have a *crescendo* towards the C, with each similar subsequent phrase similarly shaped, building up in dynamic to bar 31.

This is an unusual and vibrant addition to the repertoire.

C:2 Mike Cornick *Modulations*

Many of us have, at some time in our career, yearned to be able to sit at the piano and spontaneously improvise some seductive jazz. If we can't improvise, then here is the next best thing. The only word of caution is that it must *sound* improvised.

A 'cool' swung count-in (a-1, a-2, a-1-2-3-4) and a slow nod of the head or roll of the shoulders will help the feel, as will a very relaxed beat and smoochy *legato* tone. Let the harmonies do the work and keep the dynamics well down as marked.

The notes are not technically difficult to play, but it is the idiom that will elude many pupils. Examiners often hear jazz played like Beethoven or Brahms and it is really only by listening to a lot of blues and getting aurally and physically comfortable with the music that a pupil can expect to be able to play it with conviction. It needs to get into the blood, as it were.

As a quick teaching guide: Stage 1: Listen to lots of CDs. Stage 2: 'Move and groove' to the music; no inhibitions allowed. Use the CDs to get the physical feel of relaxation and swing. Stage 3: Some scat singing over the top of the CDs or putting 'Gershwinesque' words to the melody. Stage 4: Imitate small sections of piano solos from the CDs. And only then…Stage 5: Playing.

Notice the offbeat accents marked in bars 3 and 4. These are a feature of the style and should be used elsewhere as appropriate (top A in bar 12 perhaps). Having a swing groove playing will always help and if you do not have a resident drummer then use a rhythm from an electronic keyboard.

Most of your pupils will instinctively swing the quavers, but sometimes even minims held through a swing rhythm have a different feel to minims held through a 'straight-eight' count, so keep the triplet feel throughout.

Use plenty of pedal, changing with the harmonies, lots of rhythmic flexibility and bags of dynamic variety and changes of pianistic colour – from the most velvety and whispering of asides to a gusty, heart-rending *forte*. Enjoy this.

C:3 Khachaturian *Legend*

Anguished sighs are heard as the wind blows gently through the dark forest; the trapped soul of a beautiful maiden or handsome prince is forever imprisoned in one of the old, gnarled trees. As you approach, the sighs become a cry for help to release the spirit from its earthly confines but there is nothing you can do.

Of course this is just one version of the legend, but only with a vivid picture will the piece possess the colour and imagery it needs to convince the audience. It is a wonderful composition, full of opportunities for the exploration of different sounds, and most pupils will grow to love its haunting and soulful character as it tells its story.

It may well need some 'telling' initially from the teacher, as the harmonic language will be rather alien to many pupils. It is not technically difficult though. There are some awkward moves of the hand at times (left hand, bar 1 for instance) and hands cross over in bars 9 and 11 (right hand over left hand). The right-hand semiquavers will need to be judged carefully; place a little more emphasis on the chords rather than on the single notes to give a sense of musical line, and make a feature of the left-hand couplet phrasing. Once the chord patterns are learnt, though, and the hands begin to move instinctively from one position to another, there is little to trouble most students.

The effectiveness of the piece will be in conveying the drama. Observe all of Khachaturian's dynamic markings and don't hold back in their execution. A very obvious *crescendo* through the first two bars, a rich, mournful tenor tune in bar 9 and sharp accents in bar 10 for the wicked laughter are all examples of how the music can be given identity and purpose.

Most importantly, don't leave the expressive considerations until the notes are learnt. This is the surest way to destroy the legend for the pupil. It is the exploration of the sound world that will inspire pupils to learn the notes and do the technical work, so begin straightaway.

Pedalling will be another important consideration. Do use it in the opening, perhaps changing on the third beat, and explore its use elsewhere, particularly to enhance the phrasing. Avoid over-pedalling, however, as the piece could become rather impressionistic if it is used indiscriminately.

C:4 Richard Rodney Bennett *Taking a line for a walk*

Teachers often say 'imagine this without bar lines' to help pupils gain a smooth flow in their playing, but here the quavers make their way across the page with no time-signature or divisions to give a pulse. It looks strange, but the even quavers have a pattern and, providing they are all the same length (and the rests are also exact), the music falls into groups of 3/2, 3/2, 3/4, finding a shape and structure in an unconventional but regular way.

Each hand plays the same notes two octaves apart, so the learning time should be quite short, and the composer's instructions are meticulous and easy to follow. So far so good, and the tempo is not too challenging, so where are the potential difficulties?

The *legato*, especially in the right hand, does need to be beautifully connected, and the choice of fingering can't be left to chance. Gaps in the line spoil the effect, and any accidents in notes would be more obvious than in a denser texture.

Each section or phrase heads for the last note, and the dividing rests punctuate the journey. Skilful grading of the tone, with the left hand equally responsive to the dynamics, will be evident in successful performances, which will also have a relaxed, improvisatory feel around the passages containing minims – the pedal adds to the effect.

Pupils will find it easier to read the bass line when the treble climbs into the skies on the ledger lines. Hopefully, they will notice the 'octave higher' mark on the second page, a return to the usual place for the C at *loco*. From this passage to the end, the piece is at its most colourful, and as a large distance is covered on the keyboard, it would be wise to memorize the big leaps, always giving the sustained minims their full length.

It comes as rather a shock when the hands move in contrary motion near the end and this is the hardest part to manage without hitches. Even examiners hold their breath in sympathy when a good performance reaches a critical moment. Taking it easily and keeping calm will help, as the mood is quite reflective here before the final, witty exit.

C:5 L. Berkeley *Moderato*

Most candidates will be able to play within their own comfort zone in this early work of Lennox Berkeley. It has a rather French flavour, reminiscent of a village band, and is kept in shape by the left-hand 'rhythm section' chords. The cheerful but not unsophisticated melody goes on its way clearly, and with lovely contrast between the articulation of the opening figure and the *legato* line starting at bar 7. Balance between the hands will need attention, and many candidates will benefit from some detailed work on the left-hand dynamics – perhaps with the teacher playing the right hand. These repetitive rhythms could cause a uniform tonal level in the bass, whereas a real dynamic response from the left hand would add enormously to the overall polish of the performance.

The changing keys call for different tone colours and the suggested touches of pedal add sonority to significant bars, where left-hand sustained notes support the harmony. Stay away from the pedal otherwise, or the rhythm of the chords would be blurred. On the final page, the pedal continues where *simile* is printed, then the final nine bars are played with fingers only.

Part playing in the right hand from this point to the end will take some practice, until it's just as rhythmic as the single lines, and the held inner notes also need care.

The *moderato* tempo is qualified by crotchet = 112, which keeps a sense of vitality in the beat. The quaver chords are lighter than the crotchets and the different chord shapes all need to be set up so that the three notes go down exactly together.

The last page is all within a small dynamic range, so it's important to make the most of the little *crescendi* and *diminuendi* and to begin the final seven bars with enough sound in order to reach *pp* at the end. The effect is similar to a band marching, at the same tempo, into the distance until the music disappears.

C:6 Iain Hamilton *Playing with my Dog*

Nimble fingers and neat rhythm are the essential qualities required to cope with this lively little theme. Pupils choosing this one will need a crisp technique and the writing asks for equal facility in each hand.

Most of the texture is very clean – accuracy and clarity will matter, but there is a chance for a change of colour in bars 7–9 and similarly in bars 23–24 and 28–30, where *legato* pedalling would add to the *legato* connection. The detailed dynamics tell us exactly what we need to know, but pupils often miss quiet levels when the pace is on. A quick memory of the physical attack will be necessary for all the dynamics to make their point.

The trills could cause consternation, especially in the left hand. Make sure the *sforzandi* starts are rhythmic, then the rest of the trill can be much lighter, made with a small action – just keeping a buzz going while the semiquavers have the focus.

There may be some muddles with the rhythm in bar 2 and similar passages. The time values of bar 19 need care, especially as the next page is fast approaching. It's best to work out exactly where the beats synchronize: right-hand B natural with left-hand D, then right-hand C with left-hand E. The piece could easily suffer the kind of misreadings that sound acceptable and so go undetected by pupils. Rests arrive exactly when they should, and all the musical detail has something to say, so encourage candidates to search really thoroughly for all clues to the performance.

The Distinction performers will manage to sail through the technical demands with apparent ease and will still convey the quirky, exciting impact of the music with good-humoured flair.

GRADE 7

An accomplished performance of a Grade 7 programme should give real pleasure to the listener, including the examiner. The lists contain all the various technical and musical challenges that might be expected but there are choices for those whose musical instincts outstrip their fingers, as well as ideal vehicles for budding virtuosi. As ever, it is the balance of strengths and weaknesses that goes to make the overall assessment, not the level of technical difficulty of the chosen piece. Teachers and candidates will know the wisdom and value of choosing a varied programme, as the all-round progress of the candidates preparing for an exam is arguably more important than the actual result on the day.

LIST A

Intelligent work and musical decision-making are important in A1 and A4; the latter is not too demanding, but quite intricate. A2 has quite different technical demands; most will find it easier than the Bach, but the detail must be consistent. A6 will suit those with good awareness of dynamics, and proven experience with ornaments. A3 may be familiar to some pupils, but make sure they have the ability to sustain rhythm and concentration through quite a long piece.

LIST B

B1 has quite a demanding right-hand repetitive pattern, but masses of musical charm, while B4 is fairly straightforward technically, but needs sensitive use of the pedal. B5 would suit an angst-ridden teenager (or adult); it is not challenging in terms of note learning or pedalling, but needs natural musicality and *rubato*. A larger hand is helpful in B6, and a good *legato* touch. B3 is strongly atmospheric, and demanding in its use of tone colour. It also needs an ability to produce a big sound without percussive harshness.

LIST C

A real sense of performance is a tremendous asset in any list, but particularly in this syllabus. There is an immense range of mood, style and technical demands, so there's certainly something for everyone. Rhythm is vital in C1 and, in a different way, in C3, while C4 needs strong musical characterization, a sense of humour and variety of touch. This one is a little challenging technically. C2 is fresh and bright, with precision in chord playing a requirement. C5 will suit warm, romantically inclined pupils – this is a great piece, and bound to be popular. C6 looks harder than it actually is, and will suit those who enjoy showing off in performance. Begin it *long* before the exam, to achieve the right sort of confidence on the day.

A:1 J. C. F. Bach *Allegro*

Johann Christoph Friedrich was a son of Johann Sebastian and Anna Magdalena, and here he is continuing the family tradition of pieces suitable for teaching the next generation.

There is certainly plenty of character-building potential in this movement, the third of the Sonata in E. Qualities of control, concentration and stamina will be called on, as there is no let up in the stream of right-hand semiquavers during the four pages. Any tension in the arm or shoulder could become a progressive problem as the piece continues its relentless patterns. It will be important to practise 'over the distance' for several weeks before the exam. Fingering decisions need to be made early, and short, achievable sections tackled at a time, with lots of praise for well-earned improvements.

The kind of touch used is important; a connected line of sound in the right hand does not mean a full-blown *legato cantabile*, which would overweight the intricate figures and be too physically cumbersome. Keeping a light arm and feeling of being over the keys will help, and every opportunity for rotary action (as in bars 17–20) should be taken to ease any tiredness or tension. The left-hand quavers could be detached, but the left hand should copy the right hand in the semiquavers, and perhaps slur the pairs of quavers in places such as bars 24–7.

The printed dynamic plan adds colour and structure, but remember that the *forte* passages also need to be phrased. The main points lie further ahead, so the initial attack should be positive but not too much of a good thing.

Look at bars where ornaments in the right hand and semiquavers in the left could cause slowing up and general panic. Bar 7 is the first occasion, but the trill is evenly measured, fitting in exactly with the left hand. Later, in bar 16, the decoration is uneven and may be a bigger hazard. If it does not yield to patient treatment, leave it out; the rhythm is the priority.

This is for those who have a good facility, and who are calm under pressure. It's deeply satisfying when all the work pays off, and candidates should not be put off by the odd slip or two – it will be a rare event for a faultless performance to be presented in an exam.

A:2 Mozart *Gigue in G*

If you covered up the composer's name, would you guess this was by Mozart? Probably not. The Baroque title and the look of the writing don't suggest Wolfgang Amadeus, but we have no reason to doubt the authorship. Perhaps he was just copying an earlier style for amusement.

The piece gives another misleading visual impression – it looks much easier than the J. C. F. Bach sonata movement, but the practicalities of the articulation are the semi-hidden challenge. The *staccato* and slurring is essential, and also gives an impression of witty cross-rhythms when slurs link third and fourth quavers across the middle of the bars. This consistent detail provides a lot more to think about than the notes, and each hand is equally responsible for precision.

The left hand begins by taking the lower line in the treble clef in bar 2, then returns to its usual range at the end of bar 4. Then there is some right-hand part playing to negotiate in bars 5–8, after which the middle line is taken by the left hand. Although the two look quite far apart on the page, it works well on the keyboard. The slurs are more of a challenge when in an inner part, but should still be very clear, showing the quaver–crotchet pattern rather than the lifted second quaver of the opening – a subtle difference that is easily overlooked.

Bars 17–23 are the ones most likely to cause accidents in performance. The hands are quite far apart, which doesn't help safety, and as with chromatic scales, there is a problem in knowing where to look. There are no easy answers and players will have their own preferences, but it's important to do the same thing each time – the same fingering, visual angle and way of thinking, all of which lift the reliability factor.

This is music for fun – keep the dynamics crisp and bright, not too obviously emphatic at the *fortes*. Grade the tone into even phrases, with awareness of places where there are chords. These could easily be overdone, although the rests in the left hand do help to avoid a thick sound.

Feet stay firmly on the ground throughout; no pedal should be used at all. The exam pieces can be performed in any order, and this one may come off more happily if something more relaxing comes first on the day.

A:3 D. Scarlatti *Sonata in E*

There are at least four different styles of writing on just the first page of this well-known sonata. There are no further surprises in pattern or structure later, so finding a *comodo* and consistent tempo, which allows all these ideas to unfold within their comfort zone, is an important consideration. Bar 1 and bar 22, where a suggestion of trumpets and horns breaks into the reflective mood, could be the tempo setters. Try playing these two bars, then going back to the start, relating the rhythms exactly, until settling on the correct dignified, but purposeful, pace.

The first bar needs careful counting; some candidates will hurry the quavers, and the rhythm needs to be felt extremely well to keep the bars containing crotchets absolutely steady, and all the changing patterns rooted in the same pulse.

The editor suggests that this sonata should be played 'with the unhurried and undeviating gait of some slightly fantastic processional dance', and one can imagine dancers in amazing costumes and using stylized gestures.

Opinions vary as to pedalling in music of this period, and pupils may find it a great temptation when the tempo is quite relaxed, and repeated chords, such as at bars 12–18, give a sense of security. You will hear some recordings with pedal, but it takes great skill to avoid changing the texture or slightly blurring tones and semitones. Most candidates would be wiser to avoid pedal throughout. Examiners accept differing approaches to style as long as they are musically convincing, but playing for safety can never be wrong in this context.

The ornaments are not difficult to include, and there is the bonus of a moment's rest at bar 18 allowing a little freedom for the decoration. The printed suggestion over the crotchets in bar 2 could be reduced to a mordent on the beat, but playing the full trill will help to prevent any tendency to hurry these bars. Aim to give the repetition, bars 3 and 4, a different dynamic from that of the opening. Usually an echo works, but as no dynamics are printed, this is an ideal opportunity for pupils to make their own plan and write it in the copy. Blocks of sound or terraces are the usual approach in Scarlatti, changing as the patterns alter. There are plenty of possibilities; the thing to avoid is staying in the middle range for long stretches.

Although well-disguised, a minuet is the dance which provides the underlying rhythm, unifying the imaginative writing in the melodic line with the regularity of the dance steps in the bass.

A:4 J. S. Bach *Sinfonia No. 3 in D*

A lively, effervescent and cheerful three-part invention which bubbles along with a *joie de vivre*. It is a finger-twister and deviously written, but if you have a diligent pupil with good independence of fingers then this is musically well worth the effort.

The first and most important consideration is preparation. Like preparing a room for decorating, this often takes time, but it gives a more polished final result. The detail – notes, fingering, distribution between the hands and articulation of phrasing – must all be decided upon straightaway. If any of these is prepared without due attention to the other, then musical compromises will have to be made.

Fortunately, a kind editor has already considered the fingering and distribution for you, although it does dictate the phrasing in some instances. There is no perfect solution, but it all works and will enable a good degree of fluency. It will only need to be altered if the chosen phrasing is contrary to what is possible with this fingering.

The phrasing is up to you, but it should probably not be *legato* throughout; the opening subject works well detached, with a slightly longer B quaver and A quaver. The semiquavers could be in groups of eight, the first two phrased together, the others detached. All tied notes and notes longer than a quaver should be held for their full length.

Once the phrasing is decided on then plenty of slow practice in very small sections is needed to condition the response into the fingers. Consistency in all aspects is the key to reliable memory here. Couple this with aural work: playing individual voices, singing one whilst playing another etc. One excellent way of developing tonal control and independence of fingers is to take a small section and bring out each part independently, keeping the other two very quiet. With this sort of control, decisions can be made about which part is most suitable to project at any one moment, and it shouldn't necessarily always be the subject. The ideal is to be able to take the listener through a musical tour, and to have the technical command to be able to convey different aspects of the piece in each performance.

All this needs to be done within a broader conception of the piece, knowing where the larger phrases are and grading the dynamics accordingly, particularly during sequences. Encourage pupils to listen beyond the notes themselves, to shape beginnings and ends of phrases and to be aware of the harmonic implications of all the held notes.

If this sounds like a minefield, it isn't. In fact it's like a room of the finest lead crystal; it needs to be set up with care, each glass object in its perfect position to enhance its beauty. The listener can then be led through the display, delighting in the beauty, colour and light reflecting around the room.

A:5 Handel *Sonatina in D minor*

This is a bubbling and foot-tapping jig, which avoids the complicated part writing of the Bach sinfonia but poses its own questions for the performer. It is a more robust and confidence-boosting piece, but there are some awkward moments technically. Too many performances are likely to have uneven right-hand quavers in bars 5 and 7, for instance. The fourth and fifth fingers are notorious in this sort of figure for misbehaving, and the pupil will need to develop excellent control here and have the patience to practise.

As always, good, thorough preparation of the fingering and consistency will reap rewards. Each finger needs to know its job and to develop its independence, so be quite demanding over this.

It is the phrasing, articulation and tonal control that will make or break this performance, however. There are many ways it can be articulated, but avoid a four-beats-in-a-bar feel. Lighter second and fourth beats will definitely enhance the buoyancy, so in the right-hand first bar, for instance, you could phrase the first two quavers together and then play the rest *staccato*. The crotchet–quaver figures need a light short quaver, but make the second crotchet softer and shorter than the first where there are two or more such couplets in a row.

The suggested phrasing in bar 5 is fussy and may not help fluency. Try phrasing each group of three together, but grading each group dynamically to give the line overall musical shape. The final two groups of three in bar 6 could be detached to help the rhythmic energy.

There are not very many suggested ornaments, but they are worth considering. Remember that the hand needs to lighten to allow the fingers freedom to move. You may also consider a single grace note (in bar 25 and elsewhere); it can be just as effective and stylish.

The suggested dynamics are an excellent template so try them out, but consider a 'clean' copy and explore alternatives. Attention to these will help keep the mind and ear alert and this will help security, as a high level of concentration is needed throughout the piece. It should therefore also be known structurally and physically. Stumbles are often left-hand related so try practising it with the left hand louder then the right (as if it had the melody). This helps the ear understand the relationship between the hands and secure the memory.

Don't forget that, however secure the piece is at home or in lessons, once the adrenaline is pumping there may be a great temptation to begin too fast. This is a slightly arrogant and pompous jig so crotchet = 104 will work well and help keep a relaxed bounce in the hands.

A:6 Haydn *Allegro*

This is a wonderfully playful sonata movement, full of harmonic surprises and sudden changes of mood: skittishness, mock anger and a naive innocence. It is not entirely innocent of musical difficulties, however, and will challenge both pupil and teacher with the interpretative decisions that need to be made – not least about the ornaments.

It is an excellent choice for a pupil with good clarity of articulation and brightness of tone; there are no surprise moments that will prove over-demanding technically, providing fast passagework and quick ornaments are already in the pianist's armoury. If not, then begin the piece in plenty of time to develop this.

The right-hand tone needs a sprightly character which good, rounded fingers will provide, but avoid too much arm weight. The arm will need to be nicely balanced for the ornaments and the approach to the beginnings of phrases controlled to avoid accents, particularly after a jump. Keep the fingers fairly close to the key surface, and achieve a light *staccato* from here, especially in the quaver thirds.

The accompanying left hand needs a character and lightness of its own; anything too boisterous will dramatically affect the charm. It is surprising how many pupils underestimate just how unobtrusive the left hand needs to be in this sort of movement, so be quite challenging. The semiquavers present their own familiar problems, but a little more energy on the bottom note will help lighten the top and will be far less likely to intrude on the melody.

Then there are the ornaments! Even at this level the 'golden rule' still applies: if in doubt leave it out. This doesn't give permission to ignore them simply because of being unsure which notes to play, but rather if their inclusion causes some hesitation or physical tension. Credit will, of course, be given for stylishly executed ornaments. Opt for fewer notes – well-measured and melodically played – rather than more, if necessary. The trill on the C sharp in bar 3 could be four demisemiquavers beginning on the upper note or a quick three notes (C sharp, D, C sharp) lasting a semiquaver followed by a semiquaver rest. The easiest solution in bar 22 is four demisemiquavers beginning on the upper note, but a turn would be equally acceptable.

There are no dynamics written, but clearly a lot are needed and subtle changes of tonal colour will enhance the piece further. The only word of precaution is to ensure that the tone does not become too robust for the texture, although a little more sonority can be encouraged in the chords and octaves for the wonderful minor section.

Choose a tempo that will allow control and character rather than speed. Crotchet = 84 should work, and avoid any risk of labouring the pulse, particularly through the triplets – a common moment for unsteadiness.

The rest is in the mind. A positive yet characterful approach is needed, and poise as well as energy.

B:1 Delius *Prelude No. 2*

The first breath of spring, a gentle excitement and harmonic hints of Grieg – this one lifts the spirits from the opening bar.

Teachers will glance through the piece to see if the repetitive semiquavers ever relax, and, as the answer is only for bars 13–18, here is the main issue when matching the piece to the pupil. Rotary action has to be sustained almost throughout, so it's important that pupils have the technical 'knack' and can keep the action light, since the melodic lines lie in the left hand. The only textural change is where the quaver triplets give a marvellous chance to relax tension (but not the tempo) before the semiquavers return, rippling away until the end.

The tempo is all-important to the mood of anticipation – much slower than crotchet = 96 would lose the essential sparkle.

Many pupils will find the cross-rhythm in bar 2 something of a hurdle. To avoid an uncomfortable third beat here, there are several tricks of the trade which will help. Keeping the right-hand rhythm going evenly, and feeling where the next main beat comes, are absolute priorities. Practise hands together until the third beat, omit the left-hand A and D, then play the next E. This gives the framework and shows how much time is available for the rest of the cross-rhythm of 4 against 3. Spend a moment analyzing the exact fit of the note in this figure. The first notes in each hand, right-hand B and left-hand F sharp arrive together, after which nothing else coincides. Once mastered, the mathematics have to be put aside and the rhythm should flow evenly through to the next bar, with the left-hand melody singing out eloquently.

The balance between the hands will need attention: the right-hand patterns are in a bright part of the keyboard and need to be light, always accompanying the left hand. *Cantabile* tone warms up the cello-like melody, especially on the minims, which give sonority to the harmonies and balance the activity at the top of the texture.

The mood of the middle section (bars 13–18) stretches itself luxuriously, but at the same tempo. Don't miss the *piano* in bars 14 and 16, and ensure that quavers match while the dotted minims phrase the melody.

Bar 18 is safest played from memory, as are the last three bars. Here, as in other places where there are continuous semiquavers in both hands, extra pedal changes will keep the impressionistic sound without too much blurring. Hold the outer note of the last chord while changing the pedal for the final gentle F sharp. Just a lingering whisper rounds it off.

B:2 A. Grøndahl *Sommervise*

A happy coincidence links the three List B choices in the Grade 7 volume. Grieg influenced the Delius prelude, and Agathe Grøndahl was Norwegian, and studied with Franz Liszt.

This pastoral picture has a graceful pace and expressive split chords, but *semplice* advises us not to take too sentimental a line – it could sound overindulgent if there is too much *rubato*.

Many of the arpeggios contain an interval of a tenth, so hands need to cover this distance fairly comfortably, keeping the shape of the whole phrase and emphasizing their melodic top notes, without hesitations. Think of harp arpeggios – fluently and neatly making their point without being obtrusive.

It's wise to consider the semiquavers at bar 8 before settling on the tempo. The right-hand chords are background harmony, and should be played by rocking slightly towards the outer fingers and keeping the top line very *legato*. Of course the pedal helps, but the fingers should be creating the right sounds as well. *Legato* lines over the top of accompanying chords occur frequently in music of this period, and here we face this pianistic challenge from the first bar. The left hand helps by taking the lowest line, but as soon as four parts are involved the right hand has to manage alone, 'squeezing' the top notes a little more than the inner lines.

Some pedal is marked, but more could be used, providing quick skilful changes are a possibility, and that the pupil can really listen with great awareness. Some will opt to use the pedal only where marked, which works, providing the finger *legato* is well developed and projected. Pupils at this stage sometimes think that separate practice is too elementary for them. Do point out that the greatest pianists will spend time considering one aspect in minute detail, achieving the 'art which conceals art' by this painstaking route. Certainly this approach will benefit the right-hand semiquaver chords, and the projection of the inner melody which lies in the tenor part. The notes of the piece can be covered relatively easily, but the tonal management takes real skill.

Bars 24 to the end are the most demanding, and musically the most intense, while staying at a relatively quiet dynamic level. The phrasing will need a purposeful sense of direction, culminating in bar 31. Make the most of this expressive moment, perhaps using the left-hand quaver G to re-establish the tempo for two bars before drifting away with the final arpeggio.

B:3 Liszt *Kleines Klavierstück No. 1*

Liszt's song, 'Gestorben war ich', which rather baldly translated means 'I was dead', forms the basis of this deeply introspective piece. The German words fit the main melodic phrase, which begins after four bars of dreamy introduction. The opening line is almost without pulse, just setting an other-wordly atmosphere with a gentle wash of colour and indulgent pauses.

Once into the main theme, the rhythmic shape becomes more regular, and although the melody obviously exploits *rubato* to the full, we should never be left totally without an underlying pulse. The phrases have feminine endings, leaning on the penultimate note, and the music speaks and breathes like the poetry which inspired it.

As in much apparently improvisatory music, the composer has given detailed performance instructions, which create the texture, balance and essential style. Notice that some left-hand chords are marked *tenuto*, while others are gently detached. Slurs show the *legato* and help to emphasize main beats, especially when minims are joined to shorter notes.

A wonderful *cantabile* right across the range of dynamics really brings this one to life. Candidates often display a promising singing quality around *mezzo forte*, but lose it in quieter levels and become too harsh at *forte*. This will need careful awareness right from the start of the preparation.

The octave upbeat from bars 13–14 reinforces the theme, but Liszt warns us not to overdo this with *sempre una corda* and no increase in the printed dynamic level. The octaves are all that are needed for greater emphasis. The suggested finger change on the F sharp in bar 21 enables a smooth join to the subsequent E.

Cellos seem to join in with a rising left-hand melody (beginning with a faster tempo marking in bar 23), which moves passionately forward to the beginning of the climax at bar 31. Think here of a full orchestra accompanying the song, and go for maximum sonority without percussive harshness. Shoulders and arms will need to be poised but free from tension, and the *tenuto* chords just before will help to set up the right technical approach. The soft pedal comes off at this point and the melody blazes away right through to bar 34 before falling down in single right-hand quavers back to *tempo primo*. Whenever a main theme returns it needs something different from its first appearance, especially here after such an impassioned outburst. It's up to each individual to decide how the mood communicates itself to them personally. Imaginative, emotional pupils will instinctively understand that however carefully planned, the performance must come across as if being created in the inspiration of the moment.

B:4 Field *Sehnsuchts-Walzer*

The charm and humour of this alluring waltz will appeal to your pupils. It has a naive simplicity and, once the ledger lines are fluently read, it will not pose too many problems note-wise.

The essence of the character will only come to the fore with well-judged pedal and light, articulated phrasing. Listening skills will be crucial, as the effectiveness of the pedal will vary from instrument to instrument and some adjustment will be necessary. The commonly used but often not fully understood phrase 'pedalling with the ears' comes to mind.

Field's own pedalling needs to be taken with a pinch of salt. Pianos in the early 19th century did not have such an effective sustaining pedal and possessed a much lighter touch. Try lifting the pedal with the first chord in the left hand, not at the end of the bar. This will enhance the right-hand articulation and, if coupled with a much brighter second chord, will help give the dance buoyancy. Notice the lack of pedal in bars 5–6 and the indication to hold the bottom note. Played like this it gives a clear indication of the sort of sound Field wanted. Where the right hand is phrased over the bar (bar 7) lift the pedal slowly through the third beat so that it doesn't become too blurred.

From bar 9 the left hand needs a *legato* touch and, if the hand is large enough, it will greatly enhance the warmth if the lower notes or chords could be held under the subsequent quavers. This will give plenty of flexibility for pedal changes: preferably no pedal in bar 9 and a dab of pedal each beat to assist the phrasing in bar 11.

Once the first page is learnt then much of the hard work is done, as there is a direct repeat of the first section (bars 16–24); the final section has no technical surprises and, indeed, the left hand will feel quite familiar.

Balance is crucial throughout; in the left hand the pupil needs to give a little more weight to the bottom notes and lighten each chord. The right hand needs some brightness but must not appear too heavy. Attention to other musical detail will also be important, for instance the grace notes should be just that – graceful – and all the rests shown clearly; the quaver–semiquaver rest–semiquaver rhythm must not resemble a triplet; keep the semiquaver short and almost part of the next note and the *sforzando* should not be a demonstrative accent, more of an expressive 'leaning' into the note.

Experiment with the phrasing and tempo. Effective phrasing will be achieved if the hand 'dances' on the keys; keep plenty of pliancy in the wrist and allow the hand and fingers to rise above the key surface. The tempo should allow a flexibility and freedom to convey the waltz character: too slow and it will make the phrasing difficult to articulate with charm and lightness. Above all, the piece should be played with a smile and technical ease.

B:5 Glière *Sketch in F minor*

This is not a long journey through a period of one's life but one of those passing thoughts and emotions. This one instant in time is slightly angst-ridden and passionately felt; it explores the wonderful tenor register of the piano and dark, brooding sonority.

The first few bars are repeated twice throughout the piece and the middle section is essentially a sequence, so the note learning is not too challenging, nor is the pedal, which requires none of the finesse of, for instance, the Field.

The left-hand quavers want a relaxed freedom: a sweep and breadth of sound achieved by allowing lateral freedom of the wrist and playing from the surface of the keys. Dangerous moments occur with the swift changes of hand position, as on the second beat of bars 8 and 9 for instance. Any hint of an accent must be avoided here.

A natural rhythmic flexibility or *rubato* is essential to prevent the performance from becoming too angular and unyielding. The right-hand melody should be well projected with plenty of arm-weight behind the fingers, and the held notes listened to intelligently. This will be particularly significant in bars 5, 8, 9 and elsewhere, where the tone of the moving part must be graded carefully.

In bars 10, 12 and 14 show the wonderful dissonance, but be careful not to over-pedal. Change each beat and hold the chords until you are just about to play the next. The dynamic shape should be well defined and enhanced here, making lots of the *decrescendo*, almost shadowing the natural decay of the notes.

Rhythmically, don't worry too much about the four against three in bars 7, 17 and 24; if played accurately it will sound rather wooden. It is best to simply arrive at the next beat on time and allow a little freedom in between. It's easier played faster, so don't be too fussy while it is slow, as long as your pupil has some experience of the relationship between the notes. Otherwise, lots of clapping to CDs and perhaps some three-against-four scales will be necessary before introducing the piece.

The final few rests are significant. Hold the hands over the keys to help convey a continuing drama.

B:6 Janáček *A Blown-away Leaf*

A very beautiful and evocative piece which will attract the philosophers amongst your pupils as it is both pictorial and possesses a great depth of meaning; it is full of musical subtlety.

A large hand is helpful. Smaller hands may wish to take the semiquavers in bar 2 with the right hand but it is then difficult to match the balance of melody and accompaniment.

Indeed, it is the quality of tone in the melody and the balance of the 'fluttering' accompaniment which pose most of the problems in this piece. There is a danger of allowing too little sound in the melody and being left with no scope for shaping the ends of phrases. Take the *mezzo forte* in the opening as fairly full-bodied and use the *crescendos* wisely. Plenty of weight behind the fingers and an over-*legato* touch is one way of helping the shape, as it mustn't be too articulated.

The left hand must be light and unobtrusive. Experiment with a gently rolling and flexible movement of the hand across the keys, keeping the final semiquaver lighter than the first. Don't be too distracted by the notation, but make sure the pupil notices the occasional change of note (bar 10 for instance). The lower notes are all tied.

Bar 10 onwards could provide a very interesting point for discussion. The subdivision 2 + 3 implies a movement towards the third quaver of each bar, but thought of in 5/8 (the marking in early editions) the line has an expressive 'lean' into the first beat of each bar, giving a more spacious and relaxed feel. Use your musical judgement here.

The *accelerando* in bar 24 naturally leads into a trill, although this should probably not be measured. A natural movement into the chord in bar 30 is far more musical, even if the preceding bars are not exactly eight beats long (though they should certainly not be shortened!).

It may be worth reconsidering the fingering in bars 30 and onwards. Most pupils will feel more comfortable substituting 5-2 on the third quaver of bar 30, leaving 3 and 5 free to play the next two notes. Similarly, moving to the fourth finger on the second crotchet beat in bar 35 and then using the fifth finger for the G in bar 36 may help. In bar 37, 5-4 is probably better than 5-5, and do consider other alternatives for the next few bars, sorting out the distribution of the hands carefully.

The pedalling is effective and needs to be carefully observed but do not neglect it elsewhere; it will enhance the pianistic colour.

The end of the trill in bar 49 will be helped by a slight *ritenuto* and an elongated B flat as a sort of *portamento* into the final bar. Don't forget to ensure that the *da capo* is observed.

C:1 John McCabe *The Artful Dodger*

Rhythm and mood are always the priorities in successful performances. What about the right notes? However accurate the notes, the piece won't get off the ground without those two essentials, and this character sketch depends on rhythm and a sense of mischief.

Pupils may be familiar with our anti-hero of the title, from Dickens' *Oliver Twist*, but, if not, there is bound to be a naughty boy at school –

opportunistic but appealing – who can be the role model. The original character might have evaded the law, but examiners will not be deceived by wrong rhythms or a shaky sense of basic pulse.

Lots of counting in the early stages, with particular attention to the length of rests and tied notes, will pay off later. Bars 8–14 are a case in point, but the piece is full of potential rhythmic traps, and the only safe way is to keep a rock-steady crotchet beat and to really work out the detail in each bar.

When this piece appeared before in the syllabus, many performances were spoiled by too much pedal. There is very little need for pedalling – perhaps short dabs on the punchy chords such as the opening figure – but other sustained notes, such as in bars 8–14, are best done with the fingers, leaving the other lines crisply defined.

Bars 31–4 will usually need some counting in quavers to make absolutely certain that none of the crotchets or tied quavers is clipped. The professional's visual aid of vertical lines drawn through the music on main crotchet points will be invaluable in the process of learning to feel these beats.

Dynamics are vivid and immediate, with lots of quick changes from one level to another. The quietest passage starts at the *piano leggiero* in bar 19, which reappears at bar 22 and then fades to *pianissimo* at bar 27. The loudest chords are the final cadence, so the earlier *forte* should be less robust, but still full of energy.

It's important that the frequent accents throughout this piece are part of the rhythmic quirkiness, pointing offbeats as well as adding impact to chords. The spikiness of this writing beautifully captures the darting movements of the child-thief. Avoid any heaviness in the technical approach; the semiquavers are all neat finger actions, each one perfectly clear but not equally weighted.

The triumphant end suggests that the Artful Dodger gets away with it, and pupils with *joie de vivre* will identify with youth winning over authority for a change!

C:2 Martinů *It isn't bad, is it, to pick a few flowers*

Children's games, this time of a more harmless nature, also inspired Martinů in his folk music idiom. The activity of the quaver chords looks faster and more difficult than it actually is – the editorial metronome mark sets a lovely tempo which catches the pleasure of the scene without rushing uncomfortably. All the A-section, in both its appearances in this ternary form, is played without pedal, so a fairly high level of confidence in the fingers is needed, with no reassuring but unwise dabs with the right foot. The left-hand crotchets at the start of some bars nudge the harmonies into place, and it's a good plan to check that every note has its exact length, especially in places such as bars 9–10.

The chords are best felt as physical shapes rather than notes that need to coincide. The top line has clarity at all times, and points to the contrasts of articulation with attention to detail.

Poco meno and the preceding *ritenuto* relaxes the tempo into a different key, texture and mood, which begins at bar 17. *Legato* pedalling on each crotchet helps the sunny warmth of this *andante*, and the top line needs melodic definition over the rich harmonies. Candidates often phrase more successfully in single lines than they do in chordal passages. Here is a chance to show musical shaping, with the bass contributing as much as the top part. Tonal grading is important, as the luxurious texture could create too loud a dynamic level. Pedalling needs meticulous care in this B-section, and if the pedal action of the exam piano has not been thoroughly explored in an earlier item, it should be silently checked before beginning the piece.

The opening figure returns at bar 34, and of course the same tactics apply as in the opening.

Because of its exposed clarity, this piece could feel slightly precarious, prone to nervous slips and split notes under pressure. It should, however, suit pupils with good finger precision – perhaps those with smaller hands, rather than the long, flexible, but less precise fingers of some rapidly growing adolescents.

It's worth bearing in mind the title, with its implied question mark, to get to the heart of the matter, which inevitably creates the right tone quality. The sensible tempo certainly gives stability, but a sense of fun, simplicity and affection will also distinguish the best performances.

C:3 Milhaud *Sorocaba*

Here we are in Brazil, with a langorous tango going on in the background. Milhaud lived briefly in Rio de Janiero (1916–18), and obviously enjoyed the lazy rhythms of the popular dance music.

It may be South American in its inspiration, but Milhaud's performance directions have French precision, both in the dynamic shading and the tempo alterations.

First of all, set up a nice relaxed, but consistent pulse with the left hand, making sure the minims are held to support the harmonies. The editor writes 'Discreet use of the sustaining pedal is recommended, particularly in passages such as bars 17–18'. Usually two changes per bar work best, but minims should be held, or the second change will lose these lines.

It's dangerously easy to play the first right-hand chords after only a semiquaver rest rather than the printed quaver. If in trouble, pupils should count in quavers until the right rhythm is absorbed.

Fragments of a melody appear at bar 5, but it only really takes off from bar 9, when a super-*legatissimo* glides over the accompanying 'rhythm section' of the left hand.

Animez un peu – just a little more urgent and insidious – at bar 21 increases at bar 33, then relaxes briefly at bar 36. Then, another sudden *animez* and long *rallentando* (not too much, too soon) returns us to the initial tempo at bar 43. All this tempo management will take some organization. It's an essential aspect of the music, but the underlying dance rhythm also needs to give continuity to the whole structure. This is quite a subtle effect, which needs a mature overview of longer distances. It's certainly something that will impress examiners when evenly brought off in performance.

Returning to practical matters, the left hand can take the middle line in bars 17–18. The chords from bars 22–32 have to be covered by the right hand, and a relaxed hand shape, with the emphasis in the top lines, will make them a little easier to grasp. The effect should always be easy-going – no sudden percussive sounds to disturb the atmosphere. The middle parts are always gentle, especially when they are just adding harmonic support. Avoid offbeat quavers sticking out – it's the main two beats in a bar which always predominate. The inner chords from bar 33 are taken by the right hand – again just harmonies, nothing too obtrusive. The melodic lines, whether in single notes or chords, often start after a tied note or rest. Grade them smoothly, matching the first sound to the previous level.

The dance fades away during the last four bars, and the final chord seems reluctant to say goodnight.

C:4 Absil *Humoresque No. 3*

This is a comic piece conveying images of a circus act with the zaniest of clowns, custard pies and falling flat on one's back. The clumsy antics begin immediately, with the obscured first beat and the accented D sharps, first on the second crotchet and then on the fourth quaver. The first custard pie is thrown in bars 10–11, followed by high-pitched giggling.

The notes themselves will not be enough to convey the humour, but add some clearly articulated phrasing, a vivacious tempo, startling dynamics and plenty of slightly grotesque flexibility of pulse at crucial moments and the performer will soon have the audience smiling.

The left-hand *staccato* needs to be achieved from the surface of the keys with a quick finger movement and it should follow the right hand like a good accompanist. In bars 3 and elsewhere you might just want to take a little time placing the D sharp.

Bars 11–14 are not as tricky as they may appear at first sight. Keep the semiquavers well articulated and think in groups of notes. This will help clarify the hand positions. The final bar is a simple chromatic scale in both hands.

Grade the dynamics conscientiously but make stark contrasts, doing plenty of slow, performance practice in order to get used to the variety of touch needed. The brightest sound should be saved for bar 23 and similar points, and try to encourage your pupil to count through the syncopated bars – the pulse must not rush here. Pupils will be relieved to know that bar 42 and onwards is an almost exact repetition of the opening.

Sort out fingering very carefully. A fluent performance will require a very secure physical memory and every finger should be familiar with its task. Any duplicity will always show itself sometime, and it may well be during the exam.

This is another piece that needs a smile, both in the music and from the performer, particularly at the end. Even if nerves do creep in, it is worth reminding a pupil that an uneasy performance can be more than partly alleviated by this, and the performance redeemed by plenty of character.

C:5 Christopher Norton *Prelude II (Homecoming)*

A beautiful evening, sun setting behind you, your horse walking slowly down a dusty road, while you, reins in hand, look forward to warming your feet in front of a roaring fire and telling stories of your day at the ranch.

The second of the *Country Preludes* has it all and needs to sound slightly weary but contented. The ambling walk, mostly in the left hand, should keep the pulse fairly regular and provides a gentle forward movement through the piece, while the right hand weaves its way 'harmonica-like' around the shifting harmonies.

The effectiveness of the piece will depend on two things in particular: subtle pedalling and a good balance, particularly in the right-hand chords.

The pedal, where marked, works well harmonically, but the piece sounds rather dry without further touches to colour the sound. The opening two bars do need pedal, changing on the third and fourth beats, but it needs to be judged carefully so that it does not catch the grace note and (on the fourth beat) the semiquaver E. For the latter, try pedalling on just the final quaver of the bar.

Pedal is also needed on the final crotchet of bar 3 and similar bars to enable a smooth and unsnatched melodic line in the right hand; again, listen for the grace notes and try leaving the pedal up a fraction longer to give them clarity. This will work for almost every bar except for bars 23 onwards where changing each bar works well.

The texture will sound far too muddy if the top notes are not voiced carefully. Slightly more support and strength is needed in the weaker fingers to enable this clarity, particularly in the tenor register. This may need some technical work. It is the different 'feel' in the fingertips that will help the pupil memorize the fast attack needed for the projected note. Encourage them to become aware of this and of the way the finger interacts with the surface of the key so that they can reproduce the action at home.

The dynamics need grading carefully and should never be too loud. Make sure the pupil comes down again where appropriate, and allow some slight *rubato*, particularly through the right-hand semiquavers, in order to ease the way across some of the bar lines. It will also help some of the more awkward jumps.

A great piece for a summer's evening and an excuse for a bit of self-indulgent listening to John Denver or another Country singer with your pupil.

C:6 Carl Vine *Spartacus*

This rhythmically driving and chromatic toccata would make good film music, accompanying Spartacus and his army of slaves and gladiators as they marched to war.

It is an exciting piece, an excellent addition to the repertoire, and is one of those deceptive compositions that looks much harder than it really is. The main difficulties are co-ordinating the hands and stamina. Throughout the performance the whole physiology, but most significantly the arms and wrists, will need to remain relaxed, as the piece will slow and become very uneasy if any tension creeps in. Some of this tension will be psychological, so avoid words such as 'try' and 'practise hard' when coaxing pupils through the technique, as they imply too much effort.

The left hand should bounce at the wrist (almost a shake), with active fingers to achieve a bright sound. If the wrist is solid, then the movement will be from the elbow and too slow to achieve any fluency. Dropping on the first of each couplet with plenty of give at the wrist, and then lifting on the second, will achieve and enhance the right-hand phrasing.

Throughout, it is vital to know the 'fast' technique so that when the piece is practised slowly the 'fast' technique is used. If this is not done, then any slow practice will be almost useless as it will be impossible to speed up the mechanism without excessive tension or technical anxiety.

As a guide, almost throughout the sounds are achieved from slightly above the key, using gravity to help; a pupil will therefore need the confidence to leave the surface.

As with most fast and toccata-like pieces, this will need to be played virtually from memory before a sufficient tempo can be reached with adequate fluency. Jumps and hand movements need to be measured and physically rehearsed, so consistent fingering is essential, as is plenty of slow practice, with dynamics clearly graded. Once all is well, the secret to a successful performance is time and conditioning. It is not the piece to decide upon a couple of weeks before an exam.

The tempo marked (crotchet = 96) is perfect: not so fast that it obscures the articulation but not so slow that the piece loses its rhythmic energy.